CHAMPIONSHIP
LASER
RACING

Glenn Bourke

with Mark Rothfield

Fernhurst Books

www.fernhurstbooks.co.uk

First published in 1993 by Fernhurst Books,
Duke's Path, High Street, Arundel, W Sussex, BN19 9AJ

Printed and bound by Ebenezer Baylis & Son Ltd

British Library Cataloguing in Publication Data
  A catalogue record for this book is available from the
  British Library.

ISBN 0 906754 852

Acknowledgements
The author and publishers would like to thank The Laser
Centre, Banbury, England for the loan of boats and advice
on the manuscript, and Jeff Martin of ILCA for his support
and assistance with the project.

The trademarks

are the property of Performance Sailcraft Europe Ltd.

Photographs
All photographs by John Woodward except the following:
(Mark Rothfield): pages 4, 8, 11 (bottom), 14 (bottom), 15, 16,
17 (bottom), 18 (top), 22 (bottom), 23 (top), 26 (top left),
28, 30, 35 (top), 42, 43, 45 (top), 50, 80, 87, 88, 89, 95.
Yachting Photographics: cover, pages 7, 31, 41, 53, 57 (top),
73 (bottom), 85, 91.

Edited and designed by John Woodward
Cover design by Simon Balley.
Composition by Central Southern Typesetters, Eastbourne.

Contents

1 Introduction

In January 1988, just after I'd won my first Australian Laser Championship, I called a family meeting. We have these 'Big Three Conferences' whenever my career has come to a crossroad and I need parental guidance as to which direction to head.

I was really in a quandary this time. The nationals had given me a new-found confidence – I had felt fast and in control throughout – yet I didn't have a clue where I stood internationally. Deep down I felt I wanted to have a shot at a major goal, though I was reluctant to dig into my hard-earned savings for a tilt at a world title.

I can remember the ensuing conversation as though it happened yesterday. My father looked at me evenly and said: "Glenn, you only get one youth. One chance to do whatever it is you're capable of doing. If you don't take it then, the moment passes and there's no second chances . . . You will have to live the rest of your life wondering if you could've done it."

My mind was made up.

From the start of that '88 campaign I was blessed with having the right people to help me. The blokes at Sydney's Middle Harbour Amateur Sailing Club displayed wonderful camaraderie, donning their wetsuits to help me train throughout winter. None of them was going to the World Championships at Falmouth, but they were fantastic in helping me hone up.

I worked out a European schedule with two mates, Al McClure and Scott Ellis, both tough competitors on the water and great company off. Together, we were perfect examples of the 'little Aussie battler', all three of us doing it on shoe-string budgets. And in retrospect it couldn't have been better. We were hungry so we trained hard, building fitness and pace, while also improving tactically since we kept no secrets from each other.

Our introduction to the circuit was a frightening one: the Dutch nationals, with 220 Lasers gathering for the start in 25-30 knots. As the gun fired a burly Dutchman slotted in underneath me, filling a gap I'd made for myself in the start line. A gust hit and I instinctively dumped the main, the boom striking him in the back of the head. I got a lesson in Dutch obscenity that echoed in my ears halfway up the first beat!

After Holland we competed in major regattas in Sweden and England, interspersed with daily three-man work-out schedules. Then, in the last regatta preceding the World Championship, I hit my straps and took out the Belgian nationals, giving me great confidence at a crucial time.

Come the Worlds, I was handling the fickle Falmouth winds quite well, while most of the highly-fancied Europeans were struggling. My lead at the end of the penultimate heat was decidedly tenuous, with any one of the top eight still able to snatch victory. Heat 7 started in a solid 30 knots and, to this day, was the most testing race I've sailed. At some point through it, however, a wonderful surge of adrenalin flooded through my body and I was able to power to victory.

Crossing the line, knowing the crown was mine, the strange force melted into physical exhaustion and mental bewilderment. I slumped in the boat, virtually paralysed with emotion, until English coach Trevor Miller rescued me by rushing over with a congratulatory smile and a magnum of champagne. I went home a satisfied man.

A year later, however, I was pondering another predicament. Should I got for number two at Aarhuis in Denmark? I'm sure there's some self-defence mechanism built into an athlete's psyche after attaining a goal – 'Better to get off the stage now than run the risk of going out a bum'. Eventually it was replaced by a desire to prove to myself that the first time was no fluke.

This time I was better prepared with the little things that make life on the campaign road more comfortable. One thing that I hadn't anticipated, however, was that I'd become a 'benchmark' on training days. No sooner had I set myself up with a couple of training partners, than we would be swarmed by a fleet of party crashers.

The first heat saw me finish eighth; not a great result but since I'd been back at 30th place at the first mark, and passed eight boats on the last leg, I felt it could've been much worse. Consolidating from then on, it came to the last race where only one other sailor could beat me. A full-on matchrace ensued, me finishing 14th and he 20th, and as I headed for shore a feeling of relief and disbelief, but not joy, flooded my emotions.

For the 1990 Worlds at Newport, Rhode Island, I had the burning desire from the outset to win three in a row, something no other sailor had managed. The only question was whether to repeat the European schedule which had proved so successful in the previous campaigns. The temptation to go directly to the United States was strong

but I ultimately decided on the former plan, which was hard and costly but certainly necessary.

I arrived in London at 6am and by noon I had bought a car and picked up a boat. I went straight to Kiel Week, my first regatta after a lengthy enforced lay-off, and immediately felt fresh and aware in the boat. I won the event, then headed for the Dutch nationals. There I was able to train for five hours a day, getting good hiking miles into my legs – and I won the championship as well.

Next stop was the French nationals, a new ball game owing to strong currents, open waters, 180 boats and a hard-line race committee. The massive fleet was initially segregated into four groups to select which competitors could advance to the Gold division, from which the winner would be decided. I was in the third group and on two occasions caught the tailenders of the second bunch, my scores being recorded as 65 and 61, instead if 1, 1 as they should've been.

My howls of protest fell on unsympathetic ears because I couldn't speak fluent French and the race committee wasn't prepared to discuss it in English. As it turned out, my sister – who plays professional tennis in Paris – arrived in the nick of time and cleared up the matter. I made the cut-off and subsequently was fortunate enough to win the championship.

Confidence soaring, I winged my way to Newport. But there, for some reason, the wheels became shaky, if not exactly falling off. First, I got a leaky boat. Then the breezes stayed unseasonably light, preventing any decent practice. I finished a disappointing fourth in the North American titles. The next lead-up regatta was 40 nautical miles down the coast and, with no road transport available, myself and five other Australians decided to sail there. It took us eight hours, leaving my back and neck painfully stiff. Again the event was plagued by drifting conditions and I could only manage a third.

On the day before the Worlds, as if to script, the sea breeze finally arrived. It was a Godsend, as at last I could settle into a pattern. I won the first race, then adopted a conservative approach to ensure consistency, finally overcoming a strong challenge from a determined Brazilian to win in six. With the record sewn up, my body felt like a plastic bag full of water.

That night I decided to sail the final heat, though I was in the happy position of not having to. It's a wonderfully free, uninhibited, joyful feeling to sail without pressure, and I wish it could be like that always. I sailed perhaps the race of my life and as I crossed the line in first place I was hit by a swell of relief and glowing pride. My ambitions in the class had finally been fulfilled.

Everyone should have the chance to feel this good. Hopefully this book will help you achieve it.

2 Checking the boat

The Laser is a marvellous boat and fortunately it is manufactured to exacting one-design standards. Any boat made in such numbers has to have some tolerances but basically choosing a new boat is made easy by the fact that there are no 'dogs'.

THE HULL

If you're buying a used boat, check the weight of the hull. When dry, it should not weigh more than 62 kg. Look for hollows by running a straight edge (aluminium bar, steel ruler, etc.) over the hull. The first thing to check is how well the centreboard case marries into the bottom of the boat: sometimes the trailing edge can be down in comparison to the keel line, which creates drag. Second, find out if there are any depressions either side of the fin case by using the straight edge and bending a sail batten around the hull. The third common trouble spot is in the straight run towards the transom: a bump there can act like a suction cap and will tend to bog the boat down in the water.

In all my days of sailing Lasers I can't remember encountering a perfectly straight hull, but if the boat is to be used for top-level racing I'd definitely steer away from hulls with pronounced hollows.

◆ Use a straight edge to check for hollows and bumps in the hull, particularly alongside the centreboard case (left) and near the transom (right).

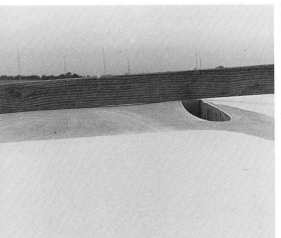
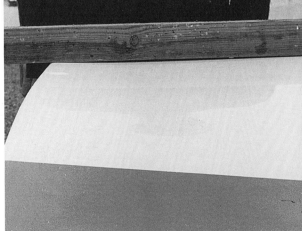

How often do you need a new boat?

Unless it is built like a battleship (and then it's no fun to sail), any boat will get tired after it has been used a lot. If you are heavy and often sail in strong winds your boat will not last as long as a boat belonging to a lightweight who sails only once a month in very light winds. An old boat can also be slightly heavier than a new one through moisture absorption, although most of this can be removed by a thorough drying of the hull through hatches.

My first boat, which I bought when I was quite young, was second-hand and had been used extensively for three seasons; it had been well looked after and had a good finish, so I was reasonably competitive at first. When the boat was five years old I felt I was losing out a little in strong winds, although still competitive in light to medium air.

I raced my next Laser very hard for three years before I started to change boats on a regular basis. A Laser lasts well compared to other small boats, but for top competition I like to renew my boat every one or two years.

The sail is actually more important than the hull. The top competitors in all international classes replace their sails every year, and some Laser sailors will buy a new boat every year just to get a new sail, because the second-hand market is so strong.

When is the boat worn out?

There are a few tell-tale signs of a tired hull. Most commonly the deck begins to delaminate, and you can detect this by running a coin or a key over the surface – you'll hear a hollow sound where the foam has come away from the 'glass. Key areas are behind the cleat on the sidedeck, usually on the outboard side, and on the cockpit floor where you've put your feet down hard.

It's not too difficult to fix: drill a series of small holes just through the laminate and inject a small amount of resin to re-adhere the foam and 'glass. It helps to be handy in the boatbuilding department or the finished product can look pretty ordinary, yet the hull can be just as strong as it was originally. But take heed: delamination is a sure indication of a hard racing life.

You can test the underwater stiffness by turning the hull upside down and physically pushing the bottom, then comparing it with a new boat. Banging with a fist is not a good indication; you should just feel with your fingers. Check the bow area, where the pressure of waves may

☛ If running a key over the deck generates a hollow sound, the deck material may be delaminating.

have caused a breakdown, and also around the fin case for star cracks.

If it feels soft in the middle, you can be sure that the hull will be 'sogging in' when going over waves rather than cutting crisply. Incidentally, a good way of increasing the longevity of a boat that's just out of the mould is to let it sit for a week to harden up.

Another obvious problem is the mast step wearing out. This can be accelerated if you rig up on the beach and get sand on the mast butt. The step will start to leak, and the more it leaks the soggier and heavier the hull will become inside. What I do is make up a tablet out of Teflon, 1 mm thick, and drop it into the hole when the boat is brand new. The downward pressure of the mast grinds it firmly into place, and I've never worn through to the gelcoat.

If you plan to keep the boat for a couple of seasons it's worth putting a couple of inspection hatches either side of the fin case so you can bolt on (rather than screw) the downhaul cleat, the mainsheet saddle, toestraps, sidedeck cleats and even the front of the grabrail, since all these can, and do, pull out or work loose.

◄ Check for cracks around the centreboard case.

◄ Fitting a couple of inspection hatches will enable you to bolt the key fittings.

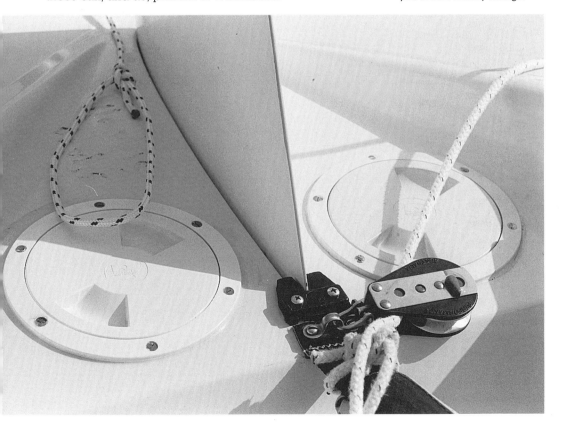

Maintenance

One of the beauties of the Laser, being fibreglass, is that it's extremely rugged. Still, all the leading sailors tend to baby their boats somewhat. The most important thing to have is a good trolley (dolly, as the Americans call them) or trailer that the boat can sit on all the time. These cradles usually consist of three prongs: a vee-shaped one at the bow and two under the gunwales just aft of amidships, keeping the load off the hull bottom.

Aussies are particularly conscious of this because our rigging areas aren't all that flash. I can go for months without my boat ever sitting on the ground, which does a lot to prevent scratches and bumps. In Europe you often see people dragging their boats up the beach or across the grass, leaning them on fences or whatever . . . and during a regatta one tiny scratch could amount to the difference between winning and losing.

Cartopping isn't too bad for the boat – it's perhaps not so good for the car – providing you strap it down properly, but you must have something soft to put the hull on when you lift it down.

If you have any chips and scratches you can fill them and sand them up again. A rub down with wet-and-dry sandpaper, followed by a buff with an electric polishing tool, will get the boat as good as new (note: polishing a hull to above the original finish is illegal under class rules).

Sometimes you get faults in the hull moulds which appear as lumps on the gelcoat surface, and these should be taken back with a sharp blade and a wet rub.

Otherwise a thorough washdown after every race is all the boat needs. When I sail in a major regatta I like to hose the boat, and dry it, after every heat to remove the residue of salt and possibly oil that's in the water. And I go over it again next morning with a clean rag so I start the day with a clean hull.

Troubleshooting for leaks

Testing for leaks is very simple. Stick some tape over the air-bleed hole below the hiking strap on the forward cockpit bulkhead. Then inflate the boat by blowing into the transom drain bung. Don't overdo it: about 20 lungfuls should be sufficient. With the hull slightly pressurised, wipe soapy water over the potential trouble spots.

We've already considered the mast step. Another place for leaks is around the top of the centreboard trunk. Some people try to quick-fix it with a blob of silicon but this tends to rub off when the centreboard comes up and down. For a long-term solution take the boat home, turn it upside down and push epoxy filler or gelcoat into the lip that forms the top of the case and down the side.

Rudder gudgeons are worth checking as they can become sloppy over the years. You may need to use bigger self-tappers or perhaps fill the screw holes and re-drill them. The bung often leaks too.

The cockpit bailer, or more specifically the join between the hull and deck where the venturi scoop comes through, can let in water with age. Often a sneaky one to detect, it should be considered when everything else appears fine. The problem is caused by the helmsman's repetitive hiking action which flexes the back wall of the cockpit, eventually leading to a break in the seal down there. The two ways to repair it are to either remove the skin fitting and gouge out the broken 'glass, or cut a hatch in the deck and bog around the area from the top.

A few boats may leak around the gunwales where there's an air void in the polyester filler between the hull and deck skins. If these go right through to the hull cavity they can suck water in at a remarkable rate, so look for them carefully, fill them and cover them with masking tape and a flowcoat of resin.

The goal, obviously, is to achieve 100 per cent waterproofing, and indeed the last four Lasers I've owned haven't taken a drop. If I do get one that leaks, I will do the aforementioned water and detergent trick. Finally, having mentioned the air-bleed hole, a word of warning. The hole is there for a reason, to release the powerful vacuum pressures that develop within the hull – you can often hear it puffing as the boat goes through chop – and it must be left open to avoid damage. It is also against class rules to block it up.

FOILS

It is absolutely essential that your rudder and centreboard are true and have a good finish. You want the water to exit off the trailing edge as smoothly as possible, and you're allowed to sand the aft third of each foil. Done carefully, you're halfway to having an efficient blade.

The boards can be affected by heat. Leave them in the sun for too long and they sag or warp. I've had it happen quite drastically, my centreboard 'melting' over a cleat one very, very hot day in Perth. To fix it, I heated the

◆ Check the foils for alignment. If they are out of line, take one of the rudder gudgeons off the transom, fill the holes and resite it (you may need to move it up or down to avoid the original holes).

◆ Slim down the grommets in the rudder case so you can tighten the rudder bolt and eliminate slop.

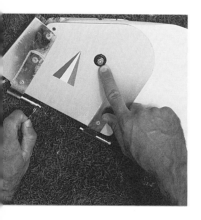

board back up with a hairdryer and deflected it as far the opposite way. Then I took the weights off and let it cool down – and fortunately the board came back perfectly straight.

Chips in the leading edge of the fins are very important as well. They say that 90 per cent of a centreboard's lift properties come from the first 30 per cent of area, so you want to make sure it's as smooth as possible. Also, because the Laser rudder is quite small and cavitates easily, it's vital to have it as efficient as possible. You know there's a problem if the rudder hums; in this case, simply sand the rudder's trailing edge with fine sandpaper and a sanding block, removing any lumps or runs. If that alone doesn't stop it, make sure that the surface of the blade is free of imperfections such as dust, scratches or an 'orange peel' ripple in the paintwork.

If you sand through the existing coating it's not a bad idea to respray the foil with polyurethane paint and repeat the sanding process. Otherwise the porous inner surface can oxidise and darken, which means the texture is rougher; it is also difficult to differentiate between these brown streaks and any weed that may be caught up when you're sailing.

Weed on the boards

The easiest way to remove kelp from the rudder, especially if it's windy and you don't want to lean aft, is to heel the boat on its ear and wiggle the tiller furiously. This tends to work the weed down towards the tip. The other way, obviously, is to ease the mainsheet and quickly run your hand down the rudder.

Both methods will slow you momentarily – for a quarter of a boat-length perhaps – but if you leave it you could lose as much as five boatlengths over 100 m of sailing. You should practise the manoeuvre so you can get back into the race as quickly as possible.

If there's weed on the centreboard too this should be cleared first. Simply zip up into the breeze a bit, pull the board right up then slam it down again. Done quickly, very minimal leeway will be made.

The rudder case

To stop the rudder blade hitting the ground when you lift the boat from the water, make sure the stock is tight. You'll notice there are two black plastic grommets either side in the middle of the plates; take them out and cut 1 mm off the side of each, and you'll find that you can tighten the

bolt a lot more. The stock will then grab the sides of the rudder, which is good for another reason in that it will eliminate slop and give a firmer feel through the tiller.

Another critical area is angle: the further back the rudder gets, the more loaded the helm becomes. Legally the limit is 78 degrees from the vertical line taken off the rudder head; any more than that will cause cavitation and a lack of responsiveness. You'll always find some weather helm, the Laser being quite a heavy boat to steer when compared with a Finn, for example, so don't expect to eliminate it completely.

Centreboard handle

I previously used the normal rope loop, but I've since been shown a better idea. It's a vertical handle, about 10 cm (4 in) long and thickly bound out of a piece of 6 mm pre-stretched rope (it looks a bit phallic!). As well as being easier to grab with one hand, its main advantage is that you can hang the loose end of the boom vang around it, preventing the rope from slipping to leeward.

Tiller jam

A shortcoming of the Laser's traveller system, particularly in the old days when stretchy braided rope was employed, is that in getting the required tension, the tiller can become jammed beneath it. It creates a sawing effect and I've gone through a lot of travellers, and many tillers, in my time.

Now, with the advent of Spectra and Kevlar rope, you don't have to tighten the traveller nearly as much to get the blocks down near the hull and still running cleanly over the tiller. Also, with the high vang loads we're carrying these days you can afford to ease the traveller rope slightly, and the boom will still move outboard laterally.

Something to remember with the new cords is that you should replace them as soon as they start to look worn, because the outer weave can fray and ball up, preventing the traveller from going across.

The tiller itself is important too. It shouldn't jut too high in the air, certainly not more than 2.5 cm (1 in) above the cleat for the traveller. Some people add an aluminium sleeve that rolls on the tiller, reducing wear, but I prefer to keep things simple; I may go through a tiller every season but that's not a big ask.

I always lengthen the tiller to protrude about 7.5 cm (3 in) past the cockpit bulkhead, which increases the leverage and thus lightens the load on the extension. I'm not a real hacker on the helm, so the smoother it feels, the better. But the downside is that the tiller can hit your leg when bearing away, so you have to find a personal happy medium.

I once used plastic tubing (conduit) for the tiller extension, and though it flexed a bit I was pretty happy with the material. Then I saw an Irish mate, who'd not performed to the best of his ability in a particular race,

My tiller and extension.

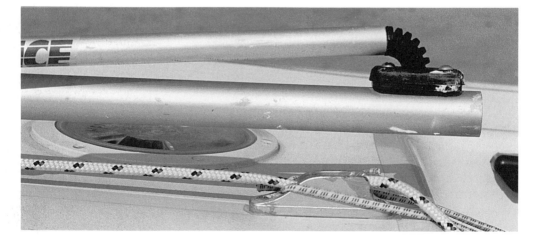

slam his extension against the deck and break it into three pieces. With one more race to sail that day he was caught short!

That proved the conduit could fail, and got me thinking that an aluminium extension might be better. I changed to it straight away, and found it also provided a more positive and sensitive feel for the boat, especially downwind when wedged in under my elbow.

SPARS

After several seasons of hard use corrosion can cause a mast to weaken and possibly break. On old masts two rivets were used to fit the mast sleeve, weakening the top section at its most heavily loaded point. All new masts use only one rivet, which should face aft. If you mark the bottom section (perpendicular from the gooseneck) and the tip, then line the rivet up, you'll find that the hole in the mast will always be in compression, rather than tension.

If you think the spar is getting a bit old and corroded you can always end-for-end it by swapping the fittings over, effectively doubling the life span. I suggest checking it at the end of each season.

Fixing a loose mast sleeve

Any movement at this joint can lead to problems down the track, not only through work-hardening but because the top section can revolve when you're pulling the sail over it, putting the aforementioned rivet out of alignment. To make sure it's a tight fit, put a bit of tape over the tip of the sleeve so it slots snugly into the bottom section of the spar.

It's not so important to have a secure fit into the mast step. I've seen people pack the hole with plastic – you're allowed a 1 mm thick strip – but I feel this prevents the mast rotating easily and can damage the boat if too tight.

Boom sleeves

Sleeving has become critical in the past few years because of high vang loads, and the length and placement have actually been written into the class rules: there are regulations dictating how far the sleeve can go into the boom and what sort of tube can be used. If you have an old boom it's well worth pulling the fittings off and inserting a sleeve. Failing that, a new boom can be made from a broken mast top section, and it won't cost anything.

◆ The distance between the plugs on the topmast is critical. The maximum measurement is 317 mm; this gives the stiffest rig, since the topmast is then at its shortest. Moving the plugs closer together gives a more flexible rig.

◄ Mark the rivet position in the topmast and align it with a mark on the aft side of the bottom mast. This ensures that the rivet hole is in compression, reducing the chance of a breakage.

Block failure

This can be a problem if they're old and worn, especially when gybing. The best way to prevent it is to take the ¾ six-gauge screws out of the Holt Allen blocks on the boom and replace them with the beefier ¾ eight-gauge variety.

Some people bolt them, but the problem here is that the bolt head sticks out so far that the blocks become less mobile and quite often catch ropes. Also, it's no good having indestructible blocks if the boom saddles can pull out, so there's a good case for bolting these as well.

Vang swivels

I use an oversized barrel swivel that can take extremely high loads; it's made by Ronstan in Australia, and Harken have a similar fitting. Either is absolutely essential for the bottom attachment, which is the best location for the cleat block to allow adjustment of the vang from any angle.

I've seen a lot of cheap set-ups, held by shackles and light pins, but these invariably break.

◆ My vang swivel.

◆ Straightening a topmast that has been bent at the join: bounce up and down on the join to spring it back into shape.

Repairing kinks

Class rules state that you can't race with a bent mast yet it's a recurring problem because of the high rig tension. Fortunately you don't always have to lash out on a new spar as the old one is easy to repair.

Quite often, almost daily in fact, I've corrected the top section by deflecting it between two trestles while it is still joined to the bottom section. The other way to do it – especially useful for bottom sections – is to employ the fork of a tree. It's wise to add a length of timber, approximately one metre (three feet) long, laid along the mast to prevent the alloy kinking at the fulcrum point when you bend it.

I sailed an entire European campaign with a bent section, repairing it every day after the race, and it didn't seem to weaken overall. Indeed I've heard the opposite said: that repeated bending can work-harden the metal – though this in turn can lead to cracking around rivet holes and the like.

Straightening a bent bottom mast: here the fulcrum (the edge of a piece of concrete) is at the point of maximum bend, with a length of timber inserted to spread the load.

SAILS

The general rule is that if a sail looks right, it is right. Since it's illegal to re-cut them, it's necessary to replace sails on a regular basis. I strongly advocate practising with reasonably good gear and racing with absolutely top-notch equipment. If you use sails that are beginning to tire and become round-backed they cause a myriad of problems, including oversteering to counter the additional weather helm, tacking through wider angles, over-use of the cunningham and reduced acceleration.

As you reach a reasonable level of proficiency it's worth rolling through sails progressively, selling them to sailors of a lesser standard if possible and buying new sails.

Longevity

At the very highest level a sail will remain at its most efficient for only four, possibly five, regattas (around 25-30 races), whereas at club level you should expect to get a season out of one, at least. I see people using the same sails year after year and they're doing themselves a great disservice; for a small outlay they can ensure their gear is on the pace and make a major improvement.

You can tell when a sail has worn out by feeling the crispness of the cloth and looking at how the battens are sitting. When a sail is new it may appear creased and angry, but the fact that the cloth is hard and resinous is good. As it ages the battens begin to hook up, giving a 'deep leech, fine entry' look to the sail – the depth is drifting aft as the mast bend takes the fullness out of the front.

Other signs are stretching and disfiguring around the downhaul eye and clew. The leech flutter also tends to get worse.

When you think about it, the Laser's Dacron sail can be its own worst enemy by automatically becoming fuller through stretching in strong winds. It's the opposite effect to what you want, and difficult to control. Despite this, I think the sail is very well designed. Sure it looks simple, but the cloth is of excellent quality and well suited to the style of rig. A more exotic sail, made of Mylar for example, would not necessarily perform better.

Finally, a fallacy exists about old sails being better to use in light airs. Sure, you can get away with it to a degree, but a new sail won't be any slower in these conditions and certainly considerably better should the breeze kick in. There's simply no reason not to use a new sail.

Setting up an old sail

If, through financial constraints, you have to persist with an ageing sail there are a few secrets to improving performance. Taking the sail to a sailmaker for alteration is not one of them, but heavy cunningham tension will go some way towards the all-important flattening: pulling the draft forward, straightening the leech and bending the mast a little more.

The rope must be rigged so that you can haul the sail eye down level with the gooseneck, which pulls a lot of

DO I NEED A NEW SAIL?

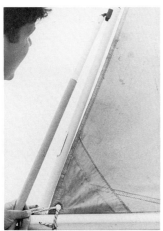

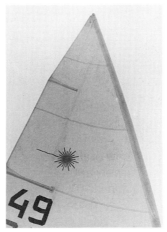

1 The leech in the clew area starts to pull out towards the back of the boom.

2 The sail develops really bad wrinkles in the head.

3 Creases up the inside edge indicate too much fullness in the back of the sail.

4 As the depth drifts aft, massive cunningham tension is needed to pull it forward again, stretching the luff.

5 Because the foot of the sail has stretched, the clew of the sail pulls out almost to the fairlead when the outhaul is tensioned.

extra cloth out. You'll also have to pull the sail foot out more than normal so that when a gust hits, the sail is already stretching to the optimum. Of course, there are times in races when you want to set up your sail on the fuller side of the mean. In light airs and sloppy waters, for example, you can obviously leave a little depth in the old sail.

Battens

Make sure your battens are straight. If they are curved there is no way of straightening them, so you will have to replace them.

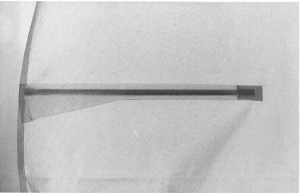

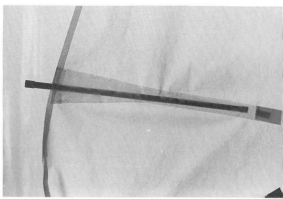

← Make sure each batten is centred on the elastic (left) or it may spring out when the sail flogs (right).

← In light airs the top of the sail should not become so deep that the weather telltale breaks; if it does, tighten the mainsheet and/or vang. But if the leeward telltale is misbehaving the top of the sail may be too flat and the boat will not gather pace, so you will need to ease the vang.

Telltales

Some people like to hang these over the sail like party streamers, but not me. I only have two: one on the panel just in front of the window, the second near the head of the sail, below and slightly for'ard of the Laser logo.

I tend to use the former as a guide for steering, say for driving deep and spinning the leeward tuft, or maybe sailing fine and heeling the boat over on top of me. I quite often shoot one eye up to check on it.

The other is a good reference for twist and head depth. What we don't want to do is set the mast up too straight in light winds, so that the top of the sail is really deep, and the top telltale will indicate this by breaking before the lower telltale. If the sail is too full, induce bend by pulling on the vang.

I personally don't use leech telltales because when I'm comfortable and sensitive in a boat I don't really need additional aids to tell me how to set the boat up. If I was to use a leech ribbon at all, I'd put it near the head as a secondary indication of depth; to show how badly the leech is stalling.

You'll find that a Laser sail will stall in light air if its draft is excessively deep: it's purely a matter of attempting to generate too much power from a relatively small sail area. Beware if your telltales are stalling more than 25 per cent of the time; your sail is too deep.

LEARNING THE ROPES

My philosophy for all the control lines aboard the Laser is simplicity – the less things to go wrong the better. That said, I still want the scope to get all the variation from the rig, so the systems must be efficient and have good range.

control	length	thickness	type
traveller	3.04 m (10 ft)	6 mm	Kevlar or Spectra
mainsheet	15 m (50 ft)	6 mm	soft 16 (or 8) plait
clew tie-down	68 cm (27 in)	4 mm	Kevlar
downhaul	3.65 m (12 ft)	5 mm	polished, pre-stretched
outhaul	4.26 m (14 ft)	5 mm	polished, pre-stretched
vang	4.26 m (14 ft)	6 mm	polished, pre-stretched

The boom vang and the cunningham are the two primary power sources for the boat, and they need to be adjusted easily and often. The outhaul, traveller and so on can be kept a little more simple. My thoughts on the various lines are as follows:

Mainsheet

This should be 6 mm polyester, in either 16-plait or 8-plait. It needs to be quite thin so it can run through the blocks easily but at the same time nice and soft in your hands. Ideal length is around 15 m (50 ft).

Vang

I use an 8:1 system for the kicker, which is very powerful but also consumes a lot of rope. You need 6 mm pre-stretched rope of the 'polished' variety – a brand like the German-made Lyros. Shiny ropes are better since they slip through blocks efficiently, and if you can't buy them you should spray the ropes with a Teflon coating – more commonly used for track slides and the like – or add a lick

◂ Tie the end of the mainsheet to the toestrap at the forward end to keep it away from your feet and out of the bailer.

◂ This vang system gives an 8:1 purchase. Note the heavy-duty swivel; the pin in the block has also been replaced with a stronger one.

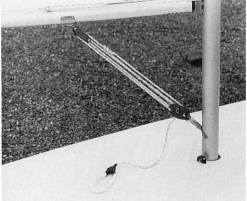

of petroleum jelly (Vaseline) around the blocks.

I have a bowline loop at the end of the vang system which is easy to grab and can be hooked over the aforementioned centreboard handle.

Cunningham

I employ two systems here, for light and heavy air. Four-to-one purchase is adequate for the former, and I prefer a 5 mm polished rope for the task. I feed it over the gooseneck pin so that the pull on the sail is direct, keeping the foot depth even on both tacks.

In heavy air I fix it at the boom vang with a loop and pass it through the sail with another loop, forming a 6:1 system which obviously requires a longer rope. I also keep it on the port side of the boom because when you come round the leeward mark it's on the weather side and thus easier to adjust. Also, it allows you to pull the sail down over the side of the boom, offering more tension if you want it.

Outhaul

I use a simple system, the rope passing through a boom cleat back to 3:1 tackle at the end, enabling adjustment during the race.

Another arrangement I've seen is a 6:1 purchase system that leads from the inboard end of the boom. With a handle attached to the end, you pull from aft and can get considerable tension, which is useful for smaller sailors. But there have been cases when the loops created by this system have fouled on the centreboard when gybing, leading to a capsize. Personally, I like to keep it simple.

← This cunningham system gives a 6:1 purchase, and is led onto the port side to make it easier to pull on at the bottom mark.

← The clew tie-down is Kevlar, with the tails tucked in so they cannot come undone. Naturally the clew needs to be as close to the boom as possible.

← The outhaul is taken around the mast and threaded through the loop of a small bowline tied in the line. The sail is at full depth when the stopper knot is up tight to the bowline.

Clew tie-down

I use 4 mm Kevlar for this, because I don't want the clew drifting too far away from the boom. Two loops around the boom and a couple of reef knots are sufficient, but I leave about 7 cm (3 in) of tail to tuck under each other, and swivel them around under the boom so they're trapped and can never come undone while sailing.

Traveller

Another basic system here, just a bowline loop passing through the deadeyes and tied off onto itself. I try to keep the loop as tight as possible because the mechanical advantage on the triangle is more efficient if kept short and tight. You'll find there's some stretch in the rope anyway.

I've adopted Kevlar rope for the traveller, usually 6 mm diameter and as smooth as possible to lessen friction on the tiller and allow the block to glide easily. The main reason for using Kevlar is that it has minimal stretch, so you can reduce the initial tension in the system.

Generally, you want the traveller block to be able to go to the outboard extension. In light airs I keep the traveller reasonably loose so the block sits up and in a little; in medium conditions I go a bit tighter again to let the block go right out; when it's heavy I ease it a fraction once again because you use so much boom vang that the block will float out to the leeward end anyway and it can clear the tiller much better if loosened.

Once I've set up the traveller for the prevailing conditions I don't touch it throughout the race. It's just not necessary to adjust it for running or whatever.

Hiking strap

I have mine fixed permanently because, being 185 cm (6 ft) tall, my legs are long enough to hike comfortably at all times with the toe-strap tightened. Shorter people have to lengthen the strap with a bit of thin cord. The problem is that when you only want the cheeks of your backside on the gunwale (e.g. for reaching) the strap is too long and your feet may get caught up with the tiller or, worse, they can slip out. You get tired, and hiking suffers accordingly.

Slouching is just the worst thing you can do as a Laser doesn't have much freeboard and your bum can hit waves. To counter that, many tend to heel the boat more and make excess leeway.

For me, the correct strap setting is where I get an equal amount of tension between my calf muscles (pressing on

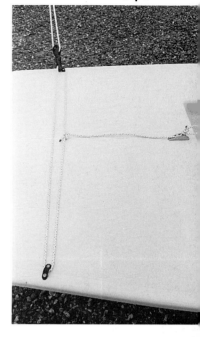

◆ Tie the bowline in the traveller so the system is already tight before the control line is tensioned.

◆ When the traveller system is tensioned it moves about this much.

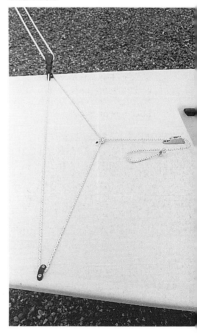

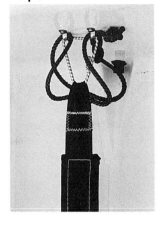

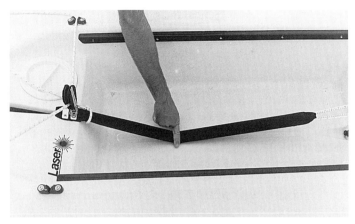

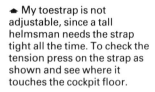

◆ My toestrap is not adjustable, since a tall helmsman needs the strap tight all the time. To check the tension press on the strap as shown and see where it touches the cockpit floor.

◆ The toestrap tension adjusted as above gives roughly equal pressure on my calf and thigh.

the edge of the cockpit) and my thighs on the deck. As well as distributing the load more efficiently, it makes my legs feel as though they're glued to the deck and any body movement relates immediately to the hull; by leaning back suddenly, for example, you can physically lift the bow.

You may like to add rubber padding around the webbing to provide some cushioning for your feet. The standard strap material has a tendency to curl up and this was painfully noticeable when I first started wearing a weight jacket, my insteps becoming badly bruised after hours of training.

I tried wearing double socks inside my hiking boots, then I found these nice straps with padding sewn on which helped greatly. A rubber tube is the worst thing you could

use as it automatically rolls the webbing and does little to spread the load around the area of your ankle which is taking all the strain.

Handles and rope loops

I think these are essential for the boom vang to help apply the amount of tension you need; they also make it easier to find. I just use two loops through a bowline, secured and tidied with electrical tape. It's quite comfy in the hand.

I use a similar handle on the tail of the outhaul, as well as the cunningham – though I don't tape this one because it needs to be undone when unrigging. Incidentally, I make these lines long enough to enable me to prop my front leg against the bulkhead and just lean back with the rope in hand, which employs body weight rather than bicep strength.

Gloves

With these narrow-diameter ropes I think hand protection is essential, but it's really personal preference. I've opted for an interesting style of glove with a stucky rubberised surface and a fabric liner; it allows me to grip the fine rope really securely, and I can also let the rope burn through the glove without chopping my hands.

Cleats

I set up my boat with the primary aim of conserving energy around the race course, because once fatigue sets in your ability to concentrate clearly on tactics and boatspeed can dwindle. Hence good cleats are essential.

A lot of early boats had plastic cleats on the cunningham, traveller and outhaul, and they tended to fail at just the wrong time. A good alloy clam cleat, such as those made by Harken and Ronstan, will last the life of the spars and hull. A system popularly practised for obtaining maximum vang – standing on the mainsheet in between the last block and the ratchet and bending the boom – used to wear out the cleats very quickly.

I've used good-quality plastic cam cleats for the mainsheet and these have proved satisfactory. Quite often there's no need to play the mainsheet, in fact if you play it frenetically you can often get out of sync. And there are many times when you need to cleat off the mainsheet so you can make adjustments elsewhere. So, despite the insistence of some colleagues that mainsheet cleats make you lazy in the sail trim department, I would not set up a boat without them.

COMPASSES

This is a topic very much open to debate, with major points ('scuse the pun) for and against. In my view, the positives for compasses are that they tell you where you're positioned in relation to the course – especially valuable when you're offshore, or in a small fleet, and don't have any reference points – and also where you are in a wind phase, and whether one end of the start line is biased.

That said, I don't use a compass on my Laser. They don't tell you what's going to happen in the next five minutes, and that's more relevant than knowing the present situation. I guess the prime reason for *not* having one is that the boat can tack on a dime. Let's assume you're in a lifting shift and there's a large number of boats on your inside: you can tack once without losing much and get halfway across to that group, then tack back again, insuring yourself against a massive failure in fleet terms. If you use a compass you may sail blindly on into the shift.

My whole regatta strategy revolves around conservatism and fleet sailing; this I do better by looking out of the boat, rather than being preoccupied by something in the boat. And I believe that when I'm honed to the upper limits of my ability I can sense phasing in the breeze.

Disregard the compass when it doesn't matter to your overall strategy. If you're covering an opponent and you both sail into a header, then stay with him. Also progressive shifts are dangerous because the compass will lie to you, telling you you're lifting but not that the boats inside you are lifting more.

◗ The excellent Silva compass simply slots into a baseplate fixed to the cunningham cleat.

What type

Should you choose to use a compass, there are a couple of good ones on the market. A Silva racing compass that's specifically designed for a Laser is one, being well damped, easy to read and removable.

Some people like tactical compasses where the numbers are cut from 36 divisions to 20, but I find the graduations are too large; a shift might look like five degrees on the compass, yet could be eight or nine degrees in real terms.

When and how often

The best time to use a compass is in the hour before the start, getting an accurate idea of how long the wind phases are, which end of the line is biased, and monitoring what side of the course is favoured.

Once on the track you can glance at the compass every so often up the beat, mostly as a positional reference; then at the top mark you can quickly work out the reach angle. But in big fleets you'll probably be more concerned with what the other boats are doing.

Another time the compass is handy is when training by yourself at an unfamiliar venue before a regatta. If you sense a geographical bend in the breeze, you'll be able to confirm it with the compass.

Boat angles

These are the most important things in my mind, dictating my tactics. I want to come off the line and get clear air first, then start looking at the angle the fleet is heading. If the boats below me are lifting, and those above are falling away, I know we're coming into a heading phase and it might be time to get out of there.

When you're really sensitive your eye is the best judge. As well as angles, your eye can tell you whether someone is in less or more wind pressure, but a compass won't.

This assumes, of course, that your pointing ability is up there with the majority of the fleet. You find in every Laser fleet that there are footers and pinchers – I fit into the latter category but I know equally proficient sailors who are the former. In the Newport Worlds which I won, the guy who came third and won three heats was very much a footer and we were both within a tiny amount of VMG (Velocity Made Good) at the windward mark on many beats.

As long as you know what you are, and what your strengths are, and can put that in the memory bank as well, then you will have a good perspective.

BURGEES

Having said that I like to keep my boat simple, this also applies to the wind indicator. I believe I can be adequately in tune with the breeze without one, and I don't want to be looking at the top of the mast when I could be looking around at the fleet and course.

A burgee is good at the start of the season when you're a bit rusty, and also downwind, highlighting changes in the angle much more sensitively than you can feel them. Most of us try to sail the shifts downwind and a burgee can be invaluable here. Remember, though, that when sailing by the lee the burgee will be indicating you're on the lifted gybe which isn't what you want to be on.

On other points I focus on the feel of the boat and the sail telltales. These will soon tell you whether you're pointing or driving, which is more relevant, and whether your sail is too full or whatever.

In any case, you are already equipped with the world's best wind indicator: your head. In major races I never wear sunglasses or a hat because a lot of the senses come from around your face and ears – and my ears are of a fairly decent size so they're pretty efficient. As an aside, Aussie America's Cup helmsman Peter Gilmour once told me he liked to cut his shirt sleeves off to feel the wind on his arms; each to their own.

The wet finger may be an old wives' tale but the wet face certainly isn't.

➤ The feel of the air on your face is your best wind indicator.

3 Setting up the rig

Starts

I always power the boat up as much as possible for the start of a race, so I can explode out of the blocks. The water around the start line is often disturbed and if you come across a patch of bad chop the boat will be able to accelerate through it more easily. Of course it means pushing the boat, hiking as hard as you can.

Should the breeze be fluctuating from, let's say, 14 to 18 knots you should set up for the lower limit; though don't go ridiculously overboard and set up for 10 knots with the foot incredibly deep. Just tweak the rig to give the maximum power level for that wind range.

● Try practising various settings on the bank. Here it was blowing at about 5 to 8 knots; you can see the effects and reproduce them yourself. For beating in light air set the mainsheet blocks about 10 cm (4 in) apart, then tighten the vang. Let off the outhaul until there is a good curve in the foot, with the sail about 23 cm (9 in) from the boom cleat, then tension the cunningham enough to smooth out the creases from clew to mid height.

Light air

You need to generate as much power as possible in these conditions and accordingly I set up the sail with a deep foot, probably 20-30 cm (8-12 in), very moderate tension on the cunningham (just enough to pull the wrinkles out of the sail but not flatten the head) and minimal vang tension.

The latter is quite critical. If you're sailing along comfortably, maybe freeing sheet a little every now and then to power over bad waves, what you must be able to do is ease the mainsheet further without creating any more depth in the sail – if you have to duck a stern or drive over somebody you don't want the vang so loose that the sail becomes deeper than the optimum setting.

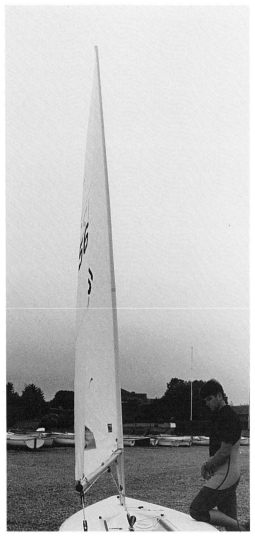

For the reaching legs ease the vang further to deepen the front of the sail, and ease the cunningham completely so the blocks are about 30 cm (12 in) apart. At the bottom mark, re-set the sail for the windward leg.

On the run, set up the cunningham and vang in much the same way as on the reach, with maybe even less tension. Pull the centreboard well up and try to heel the boat to weather. Work the small waves to accelerate down the face of them, and even run by the lee a little.

Don't let the boom too far past 90 degrees from the hull's centreline because the sail seems most efficient if the pressure is running from the leech to the luff; it tends to balance the boat nicely and it runs faster.

◆ For a light reach, ease the vang so that with the blocks 20 cm (8 in) apart the vang is just tight. The outhaul stays as it was for the beat, but the cunningham should be off.

Moderate air

Again the reaching and running settings for the vang and cunningham are similar. Ease the mainsheet blocks around 20-30 cm (8-12 in).

Depending on wind strength and how tight the reach is, you should lift the centreboard slightly (obviously the more wind or the lower the course, the less board you need). There's a fine line between having it up or down too far and, if anything, it is better to err on the side of up. As soon as you feel the hull starting to skate sideways drop it a little.

◆ For beating in medium air set up the mainsheet block-to-block, pull on the vang and overtighten it a little, then let off the outhaul until the power balance feels right. There should be a gap of about 13 cm (5 in) between the sail and the boom cleat. Tension the cunningham just enough to take out the crease from clew to mid height.

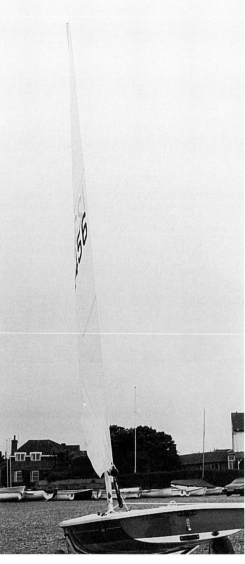

☛ For a medium-air reach, set up the mainsheet blocks 10 cm (4 in) apart, release the vang until it is just tight, let off the cunningham completely but keep the outhaul the same as for beating.

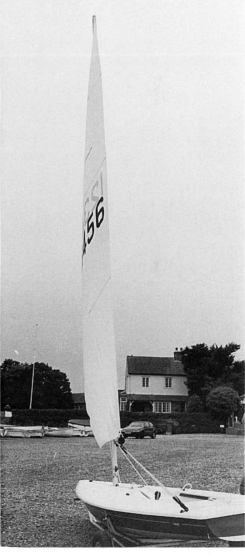

For beating in heavy air pull the cunningham so tight that the eye comes right down to the boom, or even further if the sail is old. Tension the vang so much that the boom does not move up at all when the sheet is released. Pull the outhaul fairly tight so the creases just disappear when the sail fills in heavy air.

Heavy air

This is the toughest set-up procedure because it's physically difficult to get the required rig tension for upwind sailing. I'd opt for a cunningham arrangement that allows the eye to be hauled down beside the gooseneck, to torture the sail over the side of the boom.

Keep some depth in the outhaul because the cunningham tension tends to blade the head of the sail and you need some power in the bottom so you can push through waves. If you pull the foot dead flat you'll find there's no drive at all and it's virtually impossible to keep the boat going in a seaway.

For the vang, have it sufficiently tight to allow the boom to travel out laterally when you dump the mainsheet. This confers more stability because the sail doesn't get fuller.

The safest bet for the offwind legs is to cleat the mainsheet block-to-block and ease the vang. When

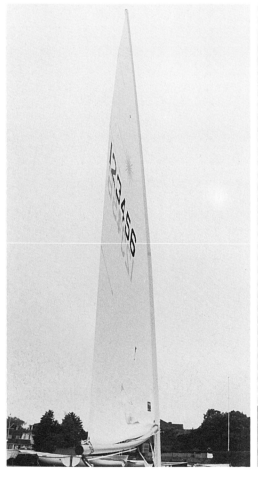

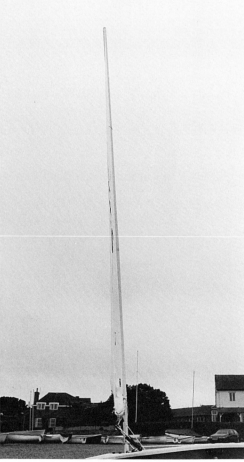

running in heavy air it's important to sail by the lee because the boat definitely becomes more stable, plus it usually eliminates the need to gybe on that leg; a high-risk manoeuvre.

I should point out that a lighter sailor would have to use more vang upwind, while a novice would use more vang downwind for extra stability, along with more centreboard. As you become more experienced and develop your boathandling, you can take a progressively more adventurous approach.

For all these settings I go by eye and feel. Marks on the various control lines might be a good idea in early days but once you get to know the boat you shouldn't need them. One mark I do find handy is a guide to the middle-point of the vang, so I know what the range is, and another on the mainsheet to indicate when the boom is at 90 degrees for running.

For reaching in heavy air set up the mainsheet block-to-block and let off the vang until it is just firm. Release the cunningham completely; this puts depth in the foot (see right) so leave the outhaul tight, as for the beat.

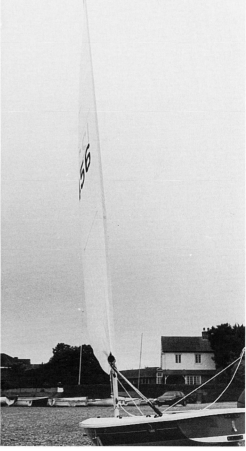

4 Fitness and training

There are two forms of exercise that apply to Laser sailing, or any physically demanding sport for that matter – aerobic, which concerns the air supply to the muscles, and anaerobic, relating to pure strength.

The former is the primary type of exercise that you'll need to do for advanced sailing. It involves high-repetition, highly-oxygenated activity such as jogging, cycling and basketball: basically anything that gets your heart rate up and generates heavy breathing and increased pulse rate to improve stamina.

Anaerobic exercise, on the other hand, involves lifting weights in low repetitions to increase muscle strength, and short bursts of energy such as sprinting: a 100 m dash takes Carl Lewis about 10 seconds (and me about twice that!) which is a relatively short time frame, so he doesn't use much oxygen.

AEROBIC FITNESS

With an aerobic activity that's designed to improve your sailing performance you need to push yourself as hard as possible. The sport I advocate for this is cycling, being leg specific but not as punishing on the joints as road running. It builds up the same muscles that you exploit when hiking, making you feel stronger for longer in the boat.

I believe every sailor should strive towards being able to hike race-long without using too much energy. This allows you to concentrate on what's happening around you; at the end of the day it should be your head, not your body, that has determined your sailing performance.

As a young pup I was a very weak hiker; it 'burnt' my legs terribly and I didn't enjoy it one bit. Frustrated, I got out of sailing for a few years, taking up competitive cycling for an outlet. When I returned to the Laser I found that hiking was a huge amount easier.

It stemmed partly from the extra strength my legs had gained during those seasons of cycling, but also because my heart and lungs had become more efficient. In short, my capacity for pushing myself had greatly increased. Aerobic fitness and stamina are not necessarily directly related, though one will help you gain the other (the

▲ Aerobic training will improve your stamina, enabling you to hike race-long without exhaustion.

longer the duration of an aerobic exercise, the more stamina you'll gain).

Laser-specific stamina, as I've mentioned, means being able to hike for a long period, and for this there's no substitute for spending time in the boat. Good fitness allows you to overcome the little problems that can crop up. For example, I once collided with another boat before the start of a major race, bumping my knee in the process. It went numb apart from a peculiar tingling sensation – like when you hit the 'funny bone' in your elbow – and I was convinced it would be impossible to get around the course.

I started the first beat hiking with just one leg and was surprised to find I had sufficient stamina to reach the first mark in reasonable shape. The feeling started to come back by the second beat, so I had one-and-a-half legs, and by the finish both were working fine.

Of course, even the fittest person may go through a pain threshold at some stage of a race and just has to punch through it. I believe it's closely related to the phenomenon of stale pain, which I equate to rust. It occurs when you've done a lot of sailing in a day, say two hard races, then have to do another – your legs feel awful at first but if you persist the pain slowly begins to dissipate.

Adrenalin, while not connected with stamina, can play a major part in improving your performance. You can get a surge of it for any number of reasons, and it should be bottled. Personally, I get it in adversity: maybe a bad error at the start that makes me go into overdrive through sheer crankiness at myself, giving 150 per cent effort for a short, sharp period. At the risk of sounding immodest, I've found myself going from the back of the fleet to within the top ten on one beat.

Adrenalin may also make you more aware of your surroundings, with your brain becoming snappier; the downside, according to doctors, is that you can feel lethargic afterwards. I guess you have to come down to earth some time; with me it's usually after the race.

BUILDING STRENGTH

You can do a lot to build your strength up before forking out the 'hard-earned' on gym fees. Cycling helps, as do sit-ups and leg raises. Also a hiking bench with the approximate dimensions of a Laser can be extremely helpful, the exercise actually being physically harder than hiking on the water. Two minutes of bench hiking equates to roughly half the first beat.

The limbs aren't the only body part that should be worked on. Obviously it's no good having limbs of Herculean proportions and an upper body as soft as sponge cake. The oft-forgotten torso takes much of the pounding, especially when you're wearing a weight jacket, so your stomach muscles need to be nice and strong to absorb the load.

Since your arms take much of the strain of holding the mainsheet and hauling on the control lines, general weight exercises for arms – bicep, tricep and forearm curls, for example – are particularly relevant.

The amount of weight you use depends on what you want to achieve. Those who want to build up their bodies should use heavier weights and low repetitions, while the average sailor would be better served by concentrating on endurance as well as strength, doing four sets of 15 in any given exercise and focussing on particular muscle groups.

You should aim to spend a minimum of two hours a day, every second day, in the gym; more if your employment allows. At my peak, in fact, I was working out for three hours every day. While not a substitute for sailing it can be a great help, especially in winter.

I highly recommend incorporating some aerobic activity in all your training. A Laser sailor needs to be a good all-round athlete, whereas in other singlehanded classes such as the Finn, competitors must be more heavily muscled; not as nimble in the boat but certainly stronger and bulkier.

Before I embarked on long European campaigns I would get my general fitness as high as I could. It's very hard to get to gymnasiums regularly once you're on the circuit, and if you do manage to you'll be inconvenienced by unfamiliar equipment and various idiosyncrasies.

As an alternative I would go jogging or swimming in my spare time, while trying to get my sailing fitness to a peak. It really takes about two months of intensive work, sailing almost daily.

Outside assistance

I've used gym partners many times and found it inspirational, getting a lot more out of myself than when training alone. A partner encourages you during the repetitions to do more, go faster etc.

Sometimes it's hard to find the right person to work out with. It's not a good idea to choose fellow competitors because rivalry can raise its ugly head in the weights room, sidetracking you from the point you're trying to reach; that is, the ultimate in personal fitness.

Body weight

I have long held that 78-80 kg (172-176 lb) is the key weight for good all-round performance, though you can certainly get away with being 76 kg (168 lb) or up to 84 kg (185 lb). Really it boils down to fitness; the smaller you are the fitter you have to be to keep up with heavyweights in strong winds. Then you enjoy benefits in light airs and downwind.

That estimation doesn't take into account the assistance of weight jackets. Some very talented European sailors swear by these jackets but I rejected them initially, being of the opinion that they'd be detrimental to my back, knees and my general health. A season in Europe convinced me it was time to give them a go.

I was surprised to find the additional burden made little difference to the way I sailed, yet improved my performance markedly. My jacket weighs three kilos (6½ lb), but they can be as heavy as five or six. The problem is you have to cut down your clothing weight, and I've seen guys with ridiculously big jackets wearing only a swimming costume and buoyancy vest in 'brass monkey' weather. That detracts from their performance in other ways – they're simply out to be 'he-men' and they forget about hypothermia and the misery of it all. On the whole it's more important to be dressed suitably for the conditions. I try to dress lightly for light conditions, and wear warmer clothing and a weight jacket for heavy air.

Incidentally, I now must wear a 12 kg (26½ lb) weight jacket to be competitive in the Finn class, giving new meaning to the word 'cumbersome'. However, if your fitness is up to scratch and you've done enough training, I'm convinced a weight jacket is an advantage, not a disadvantage, especially for sailors in the lighter weight

◆ A weight jacket (3 kg in this case) can improve your performance markedly, but only if you're fit enough to carry the extra weight.

range. I would stress that it's absolutely vital for young and lightly-built sailors to get into the gym and increase their general fitness, particularly the strength of their abdominal and thigh muscles, before taking on too much weight.

DEHYDRATION

The effect this can have on performance is well documented in sports medicine. I experienced it first-hand during the fifth heat of the World Championships at Aarhuis, Denmark. I'd been carrying a bottle of apple juice in the boat for the preceding races but the weather was quite bracing and the races had got away quickly, so I never had a chance to drink it.

Come heat five, the day was quite hot and we started having general recalls and other delays. I thirstily went to have my first sip, only to find that the apple juice had fermented into a potent alcoholic brew!

By this stage I was absolutely parched and feeling the early effects of dehydration – my clarity of mind fading, concentration lapsing and reflexes slowing. I wasn't sure whether to drink and risk intoxicatiion or take the other option and risk dehydration, so I consumed a little of the brew and suffered a bit of both. Needless to say I sailed an appalling race.

The moral? Think drinks.

The right refreshment
Despite the 'apple wine' incident, I have always favoured a drop of fresh apple juice as it's light and doesn't leave an after-taste in your mouth. I've since discovered an electrolyte-replacement beverage called Gatorade that's perhaps even better. It's important to find a drink you like because when you're uptight before the start of a race, you have to force yourself to consume it. I find soft drinks are too sweet and water too bland.

What I tend to do with any drink, be it cordial, juice or Gatorade, is dilute it to half strength, making it easier to assimilate and removing the thick syrup residue that can sometimes be left in the mouth. Gatorade is an excellent replenishment for this reason. Mixed weakly with water it has a pleasant neutral taste, quite cleansing, and restores your energy through its blend of glucose, salts, electrolytes and so on. I can noticeably feel the difference to my freshness.

You must carry a drink to prevent dehydration. A cycling bottle attached to the aft toestrap fitting is ideal for the job.

The term 'super-hydration' is commonly used by track-and-field athletes to describe the act of consuming large amounts of liquid several hours before an event. Ingesting a large amount of fluid both freshens them and enables them to go for a long period in their given event – often till the conclusion – without needing another drink.

You can try this tactic with sailboat racing to an extent, but you will need to take a secondary supply with you in the event of delays. If it's very hot, keep drinking throughout the race. If it's not, be prepared to have a 'pee' in your wetsuit!

HIKING

Having mentioned the physical side of hiking, and the fact that I like to lock myself into the deck, let's delve into the mechanics of it.

Your actual position on the boat (fore and aft) is determined by the amount of chop around. A few years ago people sat well forward, especially downwind, but the current thinking is that you should have the knuckle of the bow just kissing the water, and not digging in too much.

That means staying aft of the centreboard case at all times, and in light air you should position yourself next to the cleat. For medium air about 15 cm (6 in) aft of that would be fine, while heavy air demands that you sit roughly in the middle of the cockpit, giving you the opportunity to lean back and 'torque' the bow over waves rather than driving in.

I'm an exponent of kinetics (pertaining to movement) in sailing because it's useful for keeping the boat at the optimum angle and helping it over steep chop. That said, the abuse of kinetics can be more detrimental to

On the beat, hiking from the middle of the cockpit with your legs locked to the deck allows you to 'torque' the boat over the waves.

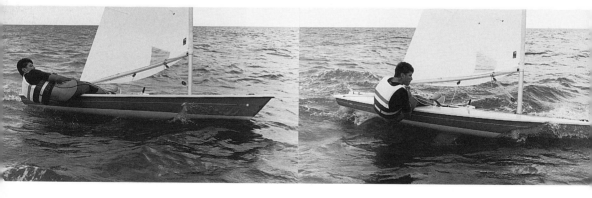

◆ When reaching, sit back with your feet forward to effectively tighten the toestrap.

boatspeed than any other factor, plus it lives dangerously within the boundaries of the rule book.

I've seen sailors power off the starting line like trains, throwing their bodies back and forth and hacking at the rudder vigorously. They can remain in sync with the conditions for maybe 100 m, but it takes very little to make them lose the rhythm and timing, and then they slow dramatically. Also, once you have a reputation for being aggressive in the boat you will surely come under close scrutiny from the race committee.

As a general rule I like to keep everything as smooth and flowing as possible, rarely attempting to jerk the hull around. If you're consistently smooth, the boat will flow along at the same pace all the time, and your occasional use of kinetics will be more subtle and still increase your speed. Remember, also, that a weight jacket exaggerates the effect of movement.

By adopting a firm hiking position on the deck and playing the mainsheet slightly it's possible to control the boat through the water without relying heavily on the rudder, which can act more as brake than an accelerator if you over-use it.

One of my all-time favourite go-fasts involves leaning the boat to weather in light airs on the beat. It gains you a few degrees of height which can be absolutely critical when boatspeed is minimal. To do it, I wedge my toes under the leeward grab rail, plant my bum on the gunwale and vary the heel to weather simply by leaning out. It sounds easy but it's quite an awkward technique to maintain – being long-legged I have to angle my feet aft in the cockpit and lean my body forward, simultaneously trying to get comfortable about having the boat apparently rolling on top of me.

➤ Heeling the boat to weather on a light-air beat is super-fast.

Finally, bad backs are a common symptom in Laser sailing – indeed it seems every sailor in the world has one – but it's not necessarily indicative of a poor hiking style. Sports medicine guys have told me that inverting the back will invariably cause problems, but I tend to hunch in the boat and still get pains. I believe it's more a muscular problem as they really do take a lot of strain. The best way to relieve it is to work on your abdominal muscles.

TRAINING

The one thing that makes for a good regatta is consistency, and this can be an extremely fragile element if you have any weaknesses in your armament. Fortunately, you can overcome any perceived shortfalls by training them out of your system: practice makes perfect.

In my case I sometimes have trouble getting up to pace when reaching and running, so I like to go for a 20-30 km (12-18 mile) run down the coast and get someone to tow my trailer to the destination. It gives me far more time on these legs than I'd normally get. Similarly, if your nemesis is heavy air, then you should go out whenever it's blowing.

The amount of time spent training depends largely on the individual, two or three hours of hard slog being average. Short and sharp is the secret. I've spent up to eight hours a day at times, but I don't see any great advantage in doing that too often. I recall watching a group of Germans train stoically before a World Championship. I thought they'd do very well, but in fact they became stale and burnt-out by it all and didn't perform well when it counted.

◄ If you capsize to leeward, hoist yourself onto the side . . .   Get one leg onto the centreboard . . .   Then the other . . .

I often practise gybing in situations I wouldn't normally be in, such as on the back of a wave with the boat parked and the mainsheet loaded. Also, I like to hold the tiller and mainsheet in one hand during the transition, repeating it several times with each hand. If you can do it then, you'll find it much easier when everything's in your favour.

Roll gybes are worth practising, since you can find out how far you can go. The same goes for heeling the boat to windward and running on the verge of wipeout.

Try to perform all your manoeuvres as fluidly and economically as possible, but not necessarily quickly. I know one sailor who looked like a very impressive boathandler but after studying him closely for a while I decided he was too flamboyant and 'physical', which detracted from his overall performance.

Capsizes

In pushing myself hard during training, I practise another important aspect: capsizing. I do this often in training, since it helps to learn how to right the boat quickly in a range of predicaments.

This proved a real bonus when I dunked it in two World Championship heats. Once was in 30 knots at the gybe mark (reasonably understandable) and the other was when square running in 10 knots! On both occasions I was able to get going again quickly, losing about 10 boat lengths but fortunately no placings.

It should be possible to recover from a leeward capsize in under 15 seconds. You should be heading for the centreboard immediately, then just flick the boat upright. A capsize to weather can be more tricky, especially if the boom is in the air, but I have a method where I swim

Lever her up and climb in as she rights.	The boat will probably be lying head-to-wind, so raise the centreboard . . .	And pull the boom to weather to swing her off onto a close-hauled course.

◄ If the boat rolls in to windward duck under the boat and pull yourself up onto the centreboard. As the boat comes up dive under the boom and into the cockpit.

underneath the gunwale and get on the centreboard to leeward. As the boat comes up I dive through the gap between the boom and deck. In the event of the hull turning turtle, treat it as a leeward capsize.

Swapping boats

Strict as the one-design concept is, I've never encountered two Lasers that feel the same. Some seem lighter on the helm, others may accelerate better and so on. Most of the time they're going at a similar speed, but the thing that can throw you is the different feel.

As mentioned earlier, one of the many boats I've owned seemed particularly fast from the word go and for some unknown reason I developed a tremendous affinity with it. Ultimately it became a pet thing, almost a superstition, so I sold it and starting rolling through hulls just as I did the rest of my gear. At the same time I borrowed as many other boats as I could to adapt to the various idiosyncrasies. This way I gradually developed the capacity to jump into any Laser and quickly get it to a reasonable pace.

It's definitely worth watching other boats to see how they're set up and how they're being sailed, though the differences can be minute. I have a fair idea of how I do things and I like to analyse this and compare it with the way others do them.

On your own

Solo practice is probably the least valuable, and least popular, of all the training options but it must be done,

particularly when you're starting out. The problem is that it can be really hard to motivate yourself. Speed training and long beats in particular seem a real chore.

If this happens set yourself a goal, or a series of goals, and strive for them; at the end of the day you should be satisfied with the amount of work you've done. I often begin with a beat of around one nautical mile and tack every 30 seconds or so; then I'll gybe as often as I can on the return run.

Group therapy

There's no question that practising with a few mates is one of the best ways of honing your racing and boathandling skills. My favourite training session involves setting up a short course, with the marks represented by a few plastic bottles attached to fishing line and lumps of lead. Up to half a dozen boats can train this way, commencing with a simple gate start, and it provides a more relevant working area.

Sail as many laps as you can until there's a definite order, then go back and start again. If you can't find a group with similar speed it's a good idea to try handicap starts. The unspoken rule is that any tactic or manoeuvre which applies in a race can be employed here, and just as you want to catch them, they'll be equally keen to block you – which means taking your wind, driving you to one side of the course and so on.

Training with one partner can also be beneficial in the early days, helping you discover tuning secrets, among other things. You can have tacking duels – useful for learning when to tack and how to cover an opponent on the last beat – plus straight-line speed can be accurately determined.

For the latter you both sail along for a set period on a single tack, starting a few boat-lengths apart and going as hard as you can. After a while, gauge who is going faster and why, make adjustments to the slower boat, then repeat the procedure until the boats become relatively even. This way, both will improve markedly.

At the end of that kind of session you should engage in some tactical and technical sailing, working shifts while trying to cover. Never get too far apart, since it clouds the evaluation.

When choosing a suitable training partner, go for someone of roughly equal speed who, perhaps more importantly, has a rational, unemotional outlook to training. After all, it can be a pretty depressing activity if one person continually gets hammered.

Don't discount training with a rival because you will most likely improve rapidly, to the point where you could both become quicker than all the others. Then you only have one sailor to concentrate on (your partner) and if you're confident in your own ability you will win the regatta.

It's not a matter of giving away trade secrets. Indeed it is essential to talk frankly about the lessons learned to gain full advantage. I like to be open with everyone, just as people were helpful to me in my early days.

◗ If you train with a partner – or even a rival – your performance will improve rapidly.

5 The race

I like to arrive at the race site up to a fortnight in advance, depending on the importance of the regatta, to arrange good accommodation and get comfortable in the environment. Every venue has its peculiarities, on the water and off, and you don't want to be distracted by this during the event. Food can be one of those problems, particularly in countries where the diet is different to what you're used to, so you should immediately locate a source of sustaining, healthy and familiar fare.

You'll also want to get accustomed to the geographical conditions that will affect the racing, and this often consumes most of the two weeks. In that time you'll get a fair idea of the predominant breezes, the consistent shifts and a few quirky aspects as well.

This formula proved successful for the three World Championships that I won. By the time each regatta started I felt completely at home with the environment and in tune with the wind phases. Significantly, very few of my rivals have been there as early. It boils down to a professional approach, and throughout my career I've prided myself on that.

PREDICTING WINDS

A lot of courses have geographic 'bends' in the true breeze which are caused by mountains, headlands, heated land masses or whatever. These effects can only be worked out by sailing the venue repeatedly beforehand. It's not a bad idea to talk to locals initially, but I tend to be sceptical about such things. Certainly the one comment you hear from fishermen and the like when a regatta starts is: "The breeze is hardly ever like this!" Personally, I like to work it out for myself, either proving or disproving the popular theories in the process.

A training partner can be invaluable during a regatta build-up, helping you to discover the ins-and-outs twice as quickly and with more accuracy than you could do alone. Once on the venue you can send your partner off in one direction while you go another for five minutes; then you both tack and converge. The boat crossing in front will have sailed the favoured course, be it due to a geographical bend, persistent shift, more breeze or whatever. Repeating this several times will give an accurate idea of percentages.

Predominant breeze

Again, it's important to get accustomed to the most likely wind throughout the event, and it pays to do a little homework before you get there.

A number of places, San Francisco or Auckland for example, are very likely to be windy, whereas one could virtually guarantee light airs to prevail on the inland lakes of Switzerland. These factors will play a big part in how you sail the boat, what weight you should be, how to set the rig up, and so on.

Concentrate on the predominant wind, but vary your approach to ensure you have no weaknesses.

System breezes

These are quite interesting, especially for Southern Hemisphere sailors such as your truly. Down under, we invariably tend to go left on a course if unsure what the breeze will do. But the global effect which determines the rotation of system breezes in the Northern Hemisphere means that right will pay dividends more often.

Countries like England are dominated by system breezes. They have three or four days of calm weather, then a system will roll through and bring an extended period of strong winds. These can be monitored by watching developments on weather maps, to the point where you can predict with a fair degree of accuracy how long it will be before the front hits, and usually how strong the wind will be.

Persistent shifts

For a conservative sailor such as myself, persistent shifts can be a real enemy. I don't sail well at venues with this phenomenon because I'm always of the opinion that the breeze will back a bit and let you get back to the middle of the course.

If the breeze doesn't back it's a matter of taking your medicine early in the race, getting to the favoured side and working the shift as it develops, preferably staying in it longer than the guy who remained on the favoured tack and then had to come in on a huge header.

At Barcelona, site of the 1992 Olympics, the oscillations can last for half an hour, which is the full period of a beat, so they largely determine tactics. You have to work out mentally where you're placed in a shift by taking compass headings or calculating what the angles should be.

As an example, let's say you've taken port-tack bearings of 240 to 270 degrees. If you round the mark and head at 240 you know you're well lifted; the chances are the breeze will head for the entire beat and you'll have to stay on the same tack. If the opposite applied, then you'd want to tack early.

Of course, a shift is only persistent in relation to the course. If your beat takes 20 minutes and the oscillations last 30 minutes then it is persistent. But if the leg took an hour it would only be an oscillating breeze.

Oscillating breezes

In most races there will generally be a couple of shifts per beat. By that, I mean major swings of 10 to 15 degrees. Inside those shifts, there'll also be wavers of five degrees or less that you won't detect on a compass; you'll only detect them if you have a good sense of boat angles among the fleet.

Chip away at these little shifts and you'll be able to stick roughly to middle ground. I always like to cover my bets, so if I have a bunch of boats to leeward I'll look for the next lift, whereas if they're to weather I will seek a header. As a general rule, however, I wait for headers before tacking back.

↞ Check the current by throwing an orange peel into the water by the buoy and seeing how far it drifts in 20 seconds. (Remember: a one-mile-per-hour current will move the peel ten metres or yards in 20 seconds.) Then eat the orange.

CURRENT

A simple way to detect tidal movement is to peel an orange and throw the skin into the water, monitoring its path alongside a fixed object such as a marker buoy. If it moves at, say, one knot per hour it can make a huge difference to how you plan your race, laylines becoming super-important.

When determining buoy positions, take land bearings where possible as you don't want to head too low, or too high, on the reach if current will affect you. For example, what seems a low route may in fact be the rhumbline.

Of course, if the tide is likely to turn during a race, you must know the exact times and alter your tactics accordingly.

THE START

The first step is to get a fix on the line, which you do simply by sighting the buoy at the far end through the flag mast of the starter vessel, or vice versa.

It can be difficult if the vessel blocks the angle, so what I do is go to the inside of the start and line up the mark with something on shore, such as a large tree or a building. This can be a somewhat imprecise science because the buoys can drift slightly, so if you're the type who sits on the line early you're taking a huge risk. There's an awful lot of people in Laser racing willing to take that risk, parking on the line with a minute to go, totally choked and trapped; sitting ducks in the sights of the race committee and thus the first to be recalled or disqualified. The usual reaction of the guys who are too early, and realise it, is to reach down the line and hit their booms against the masts of every single boat they go past, until they capsize on some unlucky sod who's been sitting there quite harmlessly.

Then there are the sailors who come reaching in late and try to punch into a hole. In a large fleet – in Lasers that can mean anything up to 220 starters – no hole exists.

My preference is for a more passive start, where you sit with the fleet and try to accelerate a second or two before them. I like to start towards the favoured end, about a third of the way down, but my primary objective is to stay out of trouble and hopefully get clear air.

By starting a little down the line, the boats to weather will obliterate you from the race committee's view in the event of a general recall, so you have more chance of geting away with being a PMS. If the race is let go then you usually have a sag to leeward of you, enabling you to roll into that gap with speed and pop away from the fleet.

High and dry

When lolling around in the countdown to the start it's best to keep the bailer shut, otherwise the cockpit can fill up within a minute.

The only exception to this rule is rough conditions, and then there's a little trick. You pull the bung off the bailer and hook it under the grab rail – it fits quite snugly if you squeeze it in – leaving the spike lying in the floor of the boat.

This stops you accidentally kicking the bailer shut or, worse, bending the pin so the unit never mates properly again. A little water may get in before the start but overall the bailer will drain far more efficiently.

More of a problem is the amount of white water that comes aboard. I've had waves wash right across the bow and slam into the back of the cockpit, stopping the boat in its tracks. One way to minimise it is to increase the angle of heel – the flatter you sail the boat, the more likely a wave will breach the foredeck. So as you approach a rogue wave poke the bow into it and heel the boat to leeward, letting most of the water run diagonally across the deck and off the side, instead of into the cockpit.

Obviously you don't want to sail the boat like this too often; the technique is only to be used for waves that are bigger than the norm.

◄ The bailer bung stowed under the grab rail.

↜ To assess the line bias, first reach down the line on port, adjusting the sheet so the luff is just full (left). Then tack and, holding the sheet in the same place, reach down the line on starboard. If the sail flaps, as here (centre), the port end is favoured. Alternatively, go head-to-wind (right) and sight across the bulkhead; if your sight line is ahead of the starboard buoy, as here, the port end is favoured.

↜ Taking a transit: here the pin lines up perfectly with a tree.

The same theory applies for the leeward end. I never start right at the pin because, while it may be biased at the time, chances are that the wind will shift back during the early stages of the beat. Also, unless they make an absolutely fabulous start, those at the pin can get hopelessly trapped by those lifting to windward.

It's not conservatism but pure common sense.

General recalls are an unfortunate fact of life in this highly competitive class. In one World Championship I contested, a heat had to be re-started 12 times and some 30 boats received their marching orders, immediately cutting the number of viable contenders given that a PMS is just the biggest waste of a race I can imagine (fortunately I've only had two in my last 300 or so races).

Through all the general recalls you have to maintain your composure and adaptability. Starting is not the clinical procedure that I may have intimated. Openings appear and close frequently as you jostle for position, and being spontaneous and instantaneous in your decisions is vital.

One final point regarding PMS's is that you should attach your sail numbers near the leech, so you can place your boat a quarter of a length in front of the guy to weather and get away with it because the front of his sail obscures yours. It could mean you get the best start in the fleet . . .

GETTING AWAY

Breaking away from the fleet is a matter of sailing fast. That sounds simple, and I know there's much more to it,

but you can achieve it providing you create a situation at
the start where you have space to leeward.

To do this, waggle your boat around and pull the bow
down to intimidate the person below you so he falls to
leeward. The next step is to slam the boat head-to-wind
and bully the weather guy away from you.

I have no doubt that a reputation helps immensely in this
situation. I found that the more success I had in the class
the fewer people wanted to start close to me. But you don't
have to be a world champion to take advantage of this;
simply find someone on the line who you know is slower
or less experienced and camp above him.

Anyway, timing is critical because you don't want
anyone trespassing on the gap you've made, so wait until
the last 20-30 seconds before the gun. With a few seconds
to go, fall off into that hole and accelerate the boat to

◆ With 203 boats in this fleet
there are no holes on the start
line to blast through.

◆ Push the boom to leeward
to stop the boat and hold your
position on the line just before
the start gun.

◆ With the boat hovering on the line, relax.

Then pull the boom to weather to fan the bow away from the wind without moving forward.

Wait, with the bow turned off the wind.

punch out of the blocks. By taking off just a bit earlier than everyone else you're guaranteed clear air.

After a good start
The moment you're clear and settled, start thinking about tactics. Where are you in the phase? Where's the fleet? Should you tack?

Your aim should be to consolidate the good position, rather than taking gambles to capitalise on it – just strive to be in the leading bunch at the first mark so you're poised to attack. If you do that in every heat you will most likely win the regatta.

After a bad start
If, God forbid, you do get buried, immediately begin to plan the most expedient and efficient exit route. It may mean working as hard as you can and waiting for things to clear, or ducking a few sterns and getting out to one side.

It's worth taking a slight loss early on, when the boats are close, to prevent an even greater loss later in the race. If negative thoughts creep in – like "I'm buggered" – you'll inevitably suffer a big deficit, so stay positive.

Something to consider in a dire situation is the bending effect that the starboard tackers create when exiting the start en masse, generating a lift for port tack. I experienced a dramatic example of this when I was sailing in a Soling worlds some time ago. We were at the pin end and got nailed by the 70 starters; the entire fleet sailed off on a starboard header, each unable to tack because of boats to weather, while we rode a port lift with

Sheet in to get the boat moving . . .

Haul in more sheet and roll the boat flat to accelerate across the line . . .

And go!

good pressure to the right of the course, came into a header which we tacked on, and rounded the windward mark in fifth place!

FIRST BEAT

Your tactics on the crucial initial beat will vary from those during the rest of the race. You should focus on boatspeed and getting into phases as quickly as possible, whereas later you may be more occupied with the opposition.

After the settling-in period, the first five minutes or so, lift your head out of the boat and look around at the fleet. You'll know what sort of phase you're in by comparing your position with those on either side.

Have you struggled to stave off the boats to leeward? If so then you'll want to consider tacking reasonably early, squeezing out the last of the lift you'll then be on.

Are you rolling over them? Then decide whether it's due to a persistent shift or whether a header will come soon. If you think the breeze is going to head, try to foot in front of the leeward bunch so that all those guys will be tucked away when the header arrives.

By being among the first to tack onto the new lift, you will also gain the upper hand on all those who have previously been to windward. So a big swag of the fleet will have been covered in the first phase, and you can do likewise to those below you on the second phase. Thus, it's imperative to take as many shifts as possible. Sometimes, however, I've sailed through shifts to get clear air, knowing the oscillations would keep coming.

That's another situation to consider. If you're not exactly where you want to be – in other words you expect either the right or left to be favoured – take the little shifts and chip away at getting there. If you tack well you'll lose very little in the process.

Ducking transoms is not a good idea at this stage. Better to persist a little longer and perhaps try to encourage others to tack. This can be achieved by pinching up and making the guy on your hip feel uncomfortable. Similarly, if you want to push someone across to one side then drive over them. Dictate the tactics – I call it manipulating the race. Of course, in these instances you must be able to dial up excellent height or blistering speed.

Port in a storm

Put simply, the right time to take the vulnerable port tack is when you won't lose too much. The wrong time is when your sole motivation is getting back to the middle of the course.

If you have to duck a number of sterns in the process it will represent boat lengths that you will never make up, and the shift can't be that great. Instead, work away until some of those guys tack voluntarily.

Quite often you can convince people to tack by yelling something appropriate, persuasive and eminently subtle such as "Can't you see we're headed? We're going the wrong way! Why don't you tack? C'mon, let's go!"

It helps if the guy thinks you know what you're talking about but, regardless, he invariably does one of two things: either gets upset about it and loses concentration, or thinks that maybe he should go.

I'm ashamed to say that on some occasions, after harassing some poor fellow into tacking, I've changed my mind and sailed on for another 50 m! That sounds like a despicable act but when you're out there to win you have to be totally selfish and look after number one. All your decisions should be based on minimising losses and maximising gains.

Upwind speed

In light air, there's a great technique where you heel the hull to weather, creating a peculiar 'upwash' off the centreboard. I'm not exactly sure why, but I assume that it forces water up the leeward side of the centreboard until it hits the hull, creating greater bit and lift. I do know for certain that it gives tremendous height.

The other advantage is that any gust will merely flatten the boat to level, whereas if you sailed it consistently upright the extra pressure would heel the boat to leeward, causing it to slide sideways.

◀ Beating in light air: the foot of the sail is loose, the cunningham is completely eased and the vang is fairly loose, having been set up with the back blocks 20 cm (8 in) apart.

◀ Note the deep foot in the sail to power it up for light air.

As the wind builds slightly hook your toes under the front of the grab rail and sit just behind the mainsheet cleat. Heel the boat to windward and push it up into the wind with the tiller. This works particularly well in flat water.

Heeling the boat to windward may feel strange, but it certainly works.

In medium conditions there are two modes to choose from – pointing or footing – depending on your tactical needs, and you set up and sail the boat accordingly. I'm assuming the rig won't require much adjustment since it won't be overpowered.

For pointing, it's obviously impossible to rake the boat to weather because your backside will drag through the water, but you should keep it as flat as possible. Keep your legs straight and your bum high out of the water.

For footing, a little heel to leeward won't hurt, plus you should start working the rudder back and forth to drive the boat through the water. The vang should be kept firm but you're able to free a little mainsheet.

Heavy air is a different ball game again. If you want to point, you need maximum vang and cunningham tensions; also, sheet the boom in block-to-block. Steer the boat positively through the swells, luffing slightly if overpressed, and throw your body outwards every time a gust hits to 'torque' the boat down. Don't dump sheet.

For footing in heavy air, the boom should remain heavily tethered by the vang so it doesn't lift when eased, thus keeping the sail flat. Free about 30 cm (12 in) of sheet and drive down with every gust. It's obviously necessary to hike for all you're worth but you can play the sheet somewhat to keep the boat on its feet.

▲ Good beating technique in medium air and flat water: straight legs and a dry bum.

◆ As the waves build, work the boat through them using your weight, the mainsheet and, if really necessary, the rudder. Leaning aft hauls the bow up and to weather; leaning forward squirts the bow down and to leeward.

Avoiding a lee bow

This is a tactical trick and a difficult one to describe, though I'll have a go. Basically, when a port-tack boat approaches on a collision course there's a good chance he'll try a 'slam dunk', whereby he tacks just in front and slightly to leeward of you.

The way to counteract this is to sail 'fat' with about four or five boat lengths to go. By that I mean bearing away a few degrees and accelerating the boat to its optimum speed: full drive mode.

The guy on port has probably already calculated how many boat lengths to go before he nails the lee-bow manoeuvre. Suddenly he'll realise that you're right on him and will become flustered, tacking immediately. The moment he tacks is your cue to round up, sheeting on and using your momentum to gain a scallop to windward.

In an instant the ball is in your court; you're a boat length upwind and gassing him beautifully, rather than him

having the advantage of a lee bow. It comes down to manipulation of angles.

The key, of course, is subtlety. If you are spotted changing your course within two boat lengths and preventing your opponent from keeping clear, you could have a case to answer to the protest committee. But short of that it's an extremely effective move.

Roll tacks

Once enormously fashionable, I believe this manoeuvre can at best gain you a little and at worst be extremely detrimental, which means it must be done expertly.

Aggressive roll tacking goes against my philosophy of keeping your actions flowing, unless your timing is excellent. Gently rolling through the tack, without dipping the gunwale, will achieve much more acceleration.

Roll tacking is of most benefit in moderate to heavy air, the physical advantage coming through getting a big fan

◄ Light-air roll tacking: lean the boat away from you, lean back as you luff up towards the breeze and then dive forward and through under the boom. Finally bring the boat up, and over to windward. Keep it fluid, or you'll lose more than you gain.

▲ A medium-air tack, with a gentle roll to fan the sail over to the weather side.

of the sail to the new weather side. But smoothness is still vital, not only for speed but because jurors are cracking down on ooching and pumping and they might start to look closely. The rules allow only two fans before you can be disqualified.

Avoiding irons

Because you are using so much vang in heavy air it can be very difficult to prevent the boat stalling in tacks. The trick is to ease about 30-45 cm (12-18 in) of sheet before the tack and go through the transition with considerable speed, pushing the helm hard over. Dive through to the new tack with the sheet still slackened and the boat driving deep.

A Laser may commonly pass through about 75-80 degrees true, but in strong winds it may be 95 degrees. The main thing is that you come out fast and accelerate promptly.

Should you muck it up, there are two ways to get out of irons. One is to pull the centreboard half up; the other is to physically pull the boom to weather, dragging the bow right around. Sail off with the centreboard partially raised and keep hiking, then once you get moving again kick the foil down with your front foot and sheet in.

Split ends

The case of a divided fleet always presents some curly possibilities. You have to rely on instinct because in covering one or other you'll be either all right or all wrong. There's no middle ground.

If your instinct says to go right, then you won't be happy going the other way. Certainly it can be very dangerous to hedge your bets and work up the centre because the fact that the fleet has split tells you the breeze is oscillating persistently. People are unsure what will happen, but at least they know it will occur over a long time frame.

Obviously, the split occurs when the leaders head in one direction and the mid-fleet batch go the other. The important point for you to determine is who is going which way and why; if some are critical to your overall strategy then you'd obviously go with them. Otherwise work it out for yourself, or even tag someone who has local knowledge.

Picking laylines

My technique for doing this is determined by my hiking position. I look over my front shoulder and when the buoy goes out of my peripheral vision I know it's time to toss.

Other people may take a different sighting point, but the angle will be the same as long as the system you use is reliable. The Laser is quite good in that there's not a huge variation between light and heavy air pointing. It tacks through around 90 degrees so it works out at roughly right angles to the centreline.

You must take into account potential shifts in the breeze and tidal influence, which is why you don't hit a layline from a long way out.

While on the subject, many people seem to get muddled up with the tiller extension when tacking and

Assessing the layline: when the buoy disappears from your peripheral vision, tack.

◆ Adjusting the vang. To pull it on, cleat the mainsheet and push against it with your foot while pulling on the vang. Then hang the loop over the centreboard handle (centre). To let off the vang, jerk it up and out of the cleat (right).

gybing. Always face forward as you come across, though this means being crossed up. As soon as you're under control, cleat the main quickly and swap the tiller to the new aft hand.

Port tackers at the mark

A common sight in any large Laser fleet is a procession of starboard tackers coming into the top mark, almost bow to stern. Simultaneously, there's a whole group of port tackers desperately trying to get on the bandwagon.

If you're on port, one way to gain access is to find a hole, but this may entail reaching and ducking sterns, which means you'll lose valuable boat-lengths. The other way is to hope the starboard line-up are overstanding. so you can tack just inside them and squeeze up to the mark.

If you're on starboard, you'll find port-tackers slamming into gaps that you couldn't swing a cat in, forcing you to either give way or tangle at the mark.

To discourage this display of arrogance and aggression, you can try the same trick with the port-tacker as you did with the would-be lee-bower halfway up the beat. Drive

down, making it look as though you're only barely laying the mark, or even struggling to. He'll believe that if he tacks under you he certainly won't make it.

As he bears away to duck your stern, use that extra speed to pinch up fine. Obviously you don't want to leave it too late, or you'll have trouble rounding, and again you can be penalised for altering course to hit him, so make the fake look convincing.

Failing that, another good idea is to yell "There's no room – don't try to get in here!"

The right tack
The safest way to approach the top mark is to join the starboard march reasonably early. However, it depends on where you're placed in the fleet, and what the wind is doing; I certainly don't advocate hitting the layline a long way out, unless on a prevailing lift.

Generally, the time to begin searching for a break is about seven-eighths up the beat. If you're out to port and have made some good gains as a result, there's always a price to pay when coming in – yet if you prepare early

◆ You need to really heave on the cunningham in heavy air. Let the sail out a bit, wait until you're going down a wave – and pull!

◆ When rounding the windward mark let the mainsheet off slightly and cleat it, followed by the vang, then the cunningham; sail round the mark and then raise the centreboard. Notice that you throw the cunningham forward so it cannot re-cleat itself.

enough the damage can be minimal. It may be worth luffing for a moment and waiting for a gap to open up rather than running to lee in search of one, though neither is ideal. The best way to do it is to lee-bow a starboard tacker yourself and force him up enough to lay the buoy.

THE REACH

Tight reaches

The way to sail this leg tactically, rather than trimwise, is to come into the mark with good speed and go *high* early. Stay high until a good set of waves or extra pressure enables you to bear away and roll over the boats below you.

If possible, keep doing it for the entire reach. You'll sail a zig-zag course, rather than the rhumbline, but there's a good chance of leapfrogging quite a number of competitors. As well as keeping your air clear, it's much easier to pick up waves.

Conversely, if you're low it can be a huge struggle just to make the wing mark.

◄ Reaching in light air. Adjust the centreboard to kill leeway; the amount will depend upon the closeness of the reach. The vang is looser than on the beat but a little tighter than the running setting.

In light air stay forward in the cockpit. Keep pressure on your leeward foot (right foot in this case) so you can come in forward and move out and back with the waves.

Broad reaches

The opposite applies on this point of sailing in that you should generally look to go *low*. Make the move soon after the mark so you can drop away deep to leeward and get undisturbed air.

The dividends come as you near the bottom mark, where you can approach at a tighter angle and with a touch more pace. This allows you to drive through the bunch that tends to collect there. Also, by being on the inside line, you will be entitled to buoy room once inside the two-boatlengths line.

If someone has the audacity to attempt a windward overtake, there are two options. The first and primary one is to let them know that while God continues to put breath in you that you will never, ever, let him or her roll you. Keep coming up and yell "Don't even think about it because we'll go to Africa!"

In medium air hook your feet forward under the strap while you are sitting back; this effectively tightens the strap, and you can either sit on the deck or hike out. Adjust the centreboard to give you the pressure you need on the tiller, and keep the mainsheet going the whole time.

◆ To squirt the boat down a wave, put your boots in the front leeward quarter and lean in and then out and back – trimming in at the same time – and jerk the rudder to pop the boat onto the plane.

Should that fail to discourage them, think about where the rest of the fleet is. If keeping one boat at bay allows six to slide through to leeward then forget it. Go back down and make sure the bulk don't get through. Remain unemotional about it.

In the reverse situation, where you're keen to roll someone else, the secret of attack is subtlety. By creeping up high early there's a chance that the victim won't notice you until it's too late. And when he finally alters his angle, you will very likely have mast abeam.

◆ As the breeze increases move back in the boat and tuck your toes under the grab rail.

Etchells 22 sailors have refined this manoeuvre into an art form, having what they call a 'passing lane'. Once a boat gets into it he can keep overtaking others all the way down the reach. It works in Lasers as well.

THE RUN

Trimming

In light air, the first step is to loosen the vang, downhaul and foot to put some bag in the sail. In addition, I trim the sail so that the breeze runs from the leech to the luff, which goes against the grain but is quite efficient in a Laser.

A common fault I see in club races is boats letting their booms way past right angles to the centreline. I have never known it to be fast; all it does is push the hull sideways to weather, whereas it should be tracking down its centreline or perhaps slipping slightly to leeward.

Heeling the boat to weather has the dual effect of reducing the wetted surface area and negating the helm

◆ On a tight reach pull the vang on a little more, push the centreboard down a bit and sit further forward to stop the bow slamming. If you are overpowered pull the cunningham on. You can pull up the centreboard if you are laying the mark, but if not then leave it down and sheet out.

▲ Running in light air: the centreboard is well up, ratchet block off, vang almost right off, cunningham off and foot of main very deep. Stay forward – but no further than middle of the centreboard. Take the sheet from the last block, hold the top of the centreboard in the same hand and heel the boat to weather.

▼ In medium air sit forward with your leeward knee pressing on the cockpit floor ready to push down if the boat rolls to weather. Use your hand and elbow as a lever on the tiller.

pressure. The speed seems to build the more the hull heels, and there is an optimum angle where the boat tracks true, the helm is light and balanced, and you can have most of the centreboard up. Unfortunately, this technique is associated with a grave risk of capsizing.

Unlike other classes which can benefit by tacking downwind on a series of broad reaches, a Laser runs square very well in light to medium airs. The only exception is when you can see more pressure on one side of the course.

Heavy air demands a slightly different approach. Basically, it's fast to run by the lee with the mainsheet trimmed some 10 degrees inside the 90-degree setting, and the breeze still running from the leech to the luff to balance the lee effect.

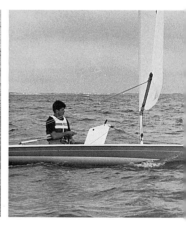

In this configuration the boat tries to roll over to weather, but you can improve the balance by burying your aft knee into the cockpit floor and leaning in, making it a whole lot safer than running dead square when the boat really starts to rock and roll. Also, you'll make good ground to leeward of the mark, often allowing you to reach to the mark and thus negating the high-risk gybe.

Backwinding is the only worry. The leech can be seen fanning in and out as a gust hits, even twisting under the pressure. However, you have to go a long way to the lee to cause a gybe. Sure it looks unusual, and it feels a little different, but it is safe and fast.

*In heavy air sit aft and run by the lee. Keep your legs forward and press down with your leeward (in this case right) foot when the boat rolls to weather. Lean into the boat, jamming your bottom into the quarter of the cockpit.

Oscillations on the run

These are just as relevant downwind as up. The thing to remember is that they're reciprocal.

As an example, let's assume you're coming into the top mark on starboard tack. You're in a lift, two minutes into the phase, on a day when you've timed the wind to be oscillating every 15 minutes. In this case, you will have around 13 minutes of headed gybe on the port run, so you'd gybe immediately.

Glance at your watch regularly to get an idea when the breeze is likely to swing back, and gybe as soon as it does; you'll sense it by the angle you're running to the course.

At the bottom mark, with a windward return to follow, it's important to remain *au fait* with the shift timing so you know which tack to take and for approximately how long.

◆ A light-air gybe, with a gentle roll to help the sail flick across.

Wave effects

Sometimes the boat will go better on one gybe than another, even though the wind is running straight down the course. What causes it is the angle of attack to the waves, which can make or break your chances of surfing them.

I've seen boats on a favoured heading gain 10 or 20 metres in no time at all, and if this happens ask yourself whether it's better pressure or a better gybe angle for the prevailing wave direction. If the latter, get onto the favoured gybe smartly.

Another telltale sign that the boat is on the wrong gybe is that the boat feels cranky, rolling incessantly and sliding from underneath you. Despite this, people commonly ignore the signs and persevere on the wrong gybe longer than they should.

When running in light airs, fix your eyes on the water behind for much of the time, searching for clean air coming through the myriad of sails. You also want to know where the cells of pressure are coming from – you can see them just as easily as when beating – since this will dictate the course sailed.

◄ Gybing in medium air.

← Rounding the leeward mark. First pull on the cunningham, and as you approach the mark push down the centreboard. Haul in the mainsheet as you round the mark. Hike, then pull on the vang.

As the wind strength builds, start to look ahead for a wave to pop the boat on. The difference between displacement speed and planing speed is, of course, enormous.

There are times when, through no real fault of your own, you sail into a windless void. Such voids occur because the pressure overtakes you, leaving the hole to descend over you. Don't get disheartened; just look for a new patch of breeze and try to make your way to it.

THE FINISH

Approaching the finish line, assess which tack will take you through the line rather than along it. A simple but important rule of thumb is to think in reverse to your starting line assessment – the favoured end of a start would be the disadvantaged end at the finish.

Many races have been won and lost at the 11th hour in simple port/starboard incidents, so where possible err on the safe side and try to come in on starboard.

It's funny, but even the calmest person can tense up towards the conclusion of the race and do irrational things. I was once in a situation where I was approaching on port, with a squadron of starboard tackers bearing down like runaway trains. I tried to tack under them and pinch through but in doing so I collected the finish mark, had to do a 360, and ultimately lost about eight places. It was a lesson I will long remember.

Be analytical. Weigh up all the options available. Keep your cool.

GENERAL TACTICS

Leader of the pack

Sailing from the front can be a curly subject. Usually only the top five or ten boats will represent a threat to you when leading, which means they're the ones to concentrate on.

On the reach you would generally stay low in order to consolidate your position. You seem to have all the options because you can accelerate down a wave when you want to, and bear up at other times. In a perfect world the rhumbline is as good as anywhere, but given any adversity I would prefer to be low.

If the second boat shows signs of going high you must maintain your clear air, and by that I mean your apparent wind which is forward of the true breeze. Don't let him get forward of it. Try to create a diagonal gap between the boats, coming up only when you have to and driving deep at all other times. It's possible to 'wiggle' your way into a handsome gain.

When you round the bottom mark sail off on the same tack, unless you're massively headed, and that helps to deceive the ensuing group into following. The last thing you want is for the fleet to split.

Sail away from the mark fast and a fraction lower than normal, and in doing so you'll give the guys behind the impression that they're onto a good thing: "He's smart so he knows which way to go, I've got clear air, and I'm pointing higher than him – What could be better?"

● Using your body weight to bounce the boat up onto the plane becomes instinctive after a while.

By giving them a bit of breathing space they'll tend to follow in single-file, each pinching up to get above you. When the next phase of breeze hits you're first into it and can wring maximum benefit, consolidating your position.

If the shoe's on the other foot, analyse for yourself whether you're lifting. If not, get outa there 'cause the guy's trying to con you!

On the last beat consider your regatta position before deciding who to cover. If the second guy has headed off on port tack and the next 10 take the starboard route, then you must weigh up whether possible victory is worth risking a poor placing, or whether you'd be better served in a regatta perspective by covering the bunch. To my way of thinking the latter is smarter, unless you're absolutely sure of a favourable wind pattern.

Never lose sight of the fact that it is a fleet race, so keep track of the other boats even when the last leg boils down to a simple matchrace with one other boat.

Steering and kinetics

These are virtually one and the same, in that you use kinetics to steer the boat. I advocate using a minimal amount of helm: I initially use my body weight to manoeuvre the hull, and if that's insufficient I will work the mainsheet; as a last resort I employ the rudder.

The kinetics involved in Laser sailing are vitally important on the beat. By throwing yourself aft you can lift the bow and pull it up to weather. Leaning forward, conversely, will make the boat bear away.

On reaches I place a foot on the bulkhead just behind the centrecase and seem to physically shove the hull forward to accelerate on to a wave. When I feel a great empathy for the boat after sailing for a long period, it seems as though I can 'unweight' myself to get the boat planing a little bit earlier than the next guy. It is a matter of bouncing the hull over a wave and cracking the plane.

The technique is more subtle than ooching, and certainly not visible to the jurors' eyes. It is an instinctive feeling and a movement, no more than a flick, that springboards the boat into weightlessness for a split second.

The big picture

You need to formulate an early game-plan, and obviously good placings in early heats help to generate a feeling of competence and confidence, whereas having to carry an early PMS or a bad placing translates into a tight 'come-from-behind' tension.

If you can get solid results in a big fleet in the first few races, it's a markedly better card than one which carries, say, two placings together with a high-points penalty heat. That means there's an axe hanging over your head for the remainder of the regatta. By heats 3 or 4, the competitors will have largely sorted themselves out, allowing that occasionally there will be an outsider who takes a flyer and wins a heat but doesn't figure prominently overall.

At that point you need to take a deeper look at your major opposition, analyse what their particular strengths are, and work out what you're going to do about them.

Peter Tanscheit of Brazil, a brilliant downwind sailor, was giving me heaps to worry about at Newport in my third and final Laser Worlds. He'd won a couple of heats but fortunately for me he'd blown out in a couple of heats. Also, my upwind speed tended to be slightly superior as I was at the peak of my fitness.

He'd come blasting at me off the breeze then I'd give him the 'blow-torch to the belly' treatment up the beats. It made for an exciting championship, but Peter's touch of wildness ultimately let him down, as he built a scorecard of the type I wouldn't advocate. He has since worked out the frailty of it because he went on to win his first world title in Greece in 1991.

Driving an opponent back

This is an oft-used, almost cliched tactic, but there are two ways to apply it – with cunning guile, or with the bluntness of a sledgehammer.

The former is far more interesting, and can be included under my motto 'manipulate the race'. In the latter stages of a regatta identify your closest rivals, then hatch a plan to bury them. This usually entails starting close to them and in a position to jump ahead of them early in the race, whether that's to leeward or weather of them on the line.

Ideally you should use shifts and make your opponents gain less advantage from them. Your cover should be merciless, forcing them to stay on a tack longer than they want, pushing them to a layline, making them do a couple of extra tacks by driving over the top near the mark. All those come under the category of manipulation and will successfully put a few boats between you.

An example of this occurred during the second World Championship that I won. A Dutch sailor had performed well throughout the regatta and was the only one in a position to beat me, so I was keen to keep track of him.

At the start there were some 95 boats at the pin end, including myself. I looked everywhere for the Dutchman to no avail, and with about three minutes to go I decided he must be at the unfavoured leeward end. As I reached down towards that end it occurred to me that if mistaken I'd be in more trouble than Speed Gordon.

Thankfully I found him hiding down there among only five other boats. But as the gun went we looked down the line and found that the boats to weather were lifting by 15 degrees and crossing us easily. A sense of despair – that "Oh no, we're buried" feeling – descended on me.

About 15 seconds after the start, however, the breeze swung our way by 20 to 30 degrees and we were now crossing the fleet by an even greater margin. The PMS gun sounded, but I remember thinking to myself that if I'd failed to find the Dutchman I could've been history.

During the 10 minutes before the next start he sailed up to me, obviously disgruntled about being found. He shouted "Do you believe in psychological games?" and I replied that I didn't; in fact I hated them. Then he proceeded to play one . . .

The previous night we'd been watching televised highlights of the Tour de France cycle race where the leader, Frenchman Laurent Fignon, had been pipped by American Greg Lemond in a sensational finish on the last day. Anyway, the Dutchman's simple slur, as we waited for the restart, was, "You're Fignon and I'm Lemond!", inferring that he would beat me and take the championship.

Until then I'd felt he was quite a nice guy and accordingly had been a little tolerant of him, but this was just the spur I needed. I immediately saw red, like never before in my life, and as I sailed away I slammed my fist into the deck repeatedly. My tolerance evaporated as I vowed to knock his lights out, metaphorically speaking.

Which I did in the next start. I quickly rolled over him and he was desperate to get clear, so he tacked onto port. I responded similarly, though there were a vast number of starboard tackers crossing us. We ducked behind 30 or so sterns, but the main thing was that I still led him.

My aim was to sail the same course he did and make it impossible for him to pass, so in effect the Dutchman called the shots as far as windshifts and fleet position were concerned. It was an extremely shifty day and it spoke volumes for his tactical ability that we recovered from mid-fleet at the first mark to the point where I finished 11th and the Dutchman 20th. Meanwhile, some guys who'd sailed their own course slipped back from the top 10 to the mid 60s.

There are many examples of psychological and other forms of aggression, from the clinical method outlined above to the infamous case which occurred during the United States' Olympic trials in 1984. There, a Finn competitor, pumped up by the knowledge that he only needed to defeat John Bertrand to gain Olympic selection, intentionally started to windward of the line to cover his arch rival. He succeeded but was ultimately blown out of the regatta. That's carrying it to the extreme.

In the reverse situation, the obvious way to break a cover is to instigate a tacking duel, throwing in the odd false tack to confuse your opponent. In doing so you'll have to be confident of outsailing him. The other way is to work the shifts perfectly – and I mean perfectly – because that means he can't be sailing them quite as well.

Cheats never prosper

There are many things you can do to gain an advantage which are legal to the letter of the law yet may be interpreted as illegal or aggressive behaviour.

One example is the aforementioned case of driving low to prevent pesky port guys burgling their way in at the top mark. Since they're trying to get away with murder, you are only playing the role of judge and juror, but it could be considered foul play in some circles.

Another situation may arise when someone is trying to pass to leeward on the run. As you approach the mark the best idea is to steer a few degrees lower, forcing the outside boat to sail a longer course than you when rounding. The rules suggest you're sailing below the proper course, but in real terms it would be impossible to prove it. Meanwhile, you've maintained control of the situation and not let him through.

Outright cheating is another matter entirely. A myriad of possibilities exist for those who are lacking a conscience, from taking the deck off and glassing it with carbon fibre to simple pumping and rocking. I've seen virtually all of them in my time, and the result has always been detrimental to the person stooping to these tactics.

If it involves an illegal modification to the boat, the helmsman is invariably ridden with guilt and fearful of being found out. More energy is expended there than worrying about tactics in the race, and this little black duck wouldn't care for it.

Rule 54, pertaining to kinetic activities such as pumping and rocking, is the most commonly exploited regulation, particularly in some of the lesser European regattas where offenders usually get off scot free. But their glory is short-lived – come the first major championship where the committee clamps down on the rule, they either have to stop the kinetic tactic and go very, very slowly, or persist and get 'pinged' for it.

I've never protested over Rule 54, yet I consider it one of the most flagrant forms of cheating. Shouting at these villains has proven effective, of not stopping them then at least putting the wind up them – if you'll pardon the pun.

Certainly, peer pressure is a powerful deterrent. What this means is that if you don't indulge in it – and you vent your spleen on those who do – quite often the fleet will realise that a standard is being set and no one will go outside the bounds. This is one of the rare occasions where the good guys get to win a round.

Collisions

My advice is to take all possible action to avoid them. The most minor 'prang' will cost you time and probably places, which will never be adequately compensated even if you're in the right – and the chances of winning any ensuing protest are mostly no better than 50:50.

In the event of collision, a decisive response is essential. As an illustration, consider what happened to me during a Pacific championship in Melbourne. We were rounding the bottom mark in about 25-30 knots of breeze when the boat immediately in front and to windward of me was bowled over by a freak wave and gust. As he capsized the leech of his sail merely flicked across the deck of my boat, but moments later he was on the centreboard and righting the boat.

I wasn't inconvenienced in the slightest, so I decided it wasn't worth protesting over. Unfortunately the guy who was directly in front of us happened to witness the collision and he called back: "If one of you doesn't do a 720-degree turn, I'll protest both of you".

We sailed on, discussing who was in the wrong – whether he was windward boat or if I had to avoid a capsized boat – and after a minute or so I hoisted a protest flag. He didn't do his turns. Come the hearing, the jury was dubious since it had taken me so long to fly the protest flag.

If they'd refused to hear it both of us would've been disqualified, simply because we'd admitted the collision.

Ultimately, they accepted it and I won. Also, I maintained that a minute was a reasonable period to decide on a protest but they held it had to be immediate.

So when in the wrong do the penalty turns immediately, while if you believe you're right just hoist the flag. The severity of the collision is irrelevant in the jury's eyes; all that concerns them is that it happened, and that they, not the competitors, should decide the outcome.

◄ Keep clear of capsizing boats; a collision could wreck your race, regardless of whose fault it is.

Sportsmanship

The action of the sailor who witnessed the aforementioned incident was, in my view, petty-minded. I know it was legal – in his own way he was manipulating the race – however it paid scant regard for sportsmanship. And without that, we're lost.

Sailors must be able to decide what is minor and unavoidable. Further, only those directly involved should be able to protest, so if you bump gunwales on the start line and no one is inconvenienced then get on with the race. For someone else to benefit from it seems totally absurd, as is the notion that one of the parties will be thrown out for such a stupid technicality.

6 Mental attitude

The yachting fraternity is deeply divided on the issue of competing in singlehanded sailboats. I have many sailing friends, whose company I enjoy immensely, who wouldn't be caught dead in a singlehander – to them it wouldn't be sailing without the mayhem and camaraderie that make up the scene on a multi-crewed craft.

When I went to Perth in 1986, seeking to crew aboard Iain Murray's 12-metre *Kookaburra*, there was a definite pecking order installed: "You're a new boy here and we've done it all before". The breakthrough didn't come easily, but I'm happy to reflect back on that period since we eventually became a wonderfully integrated team, totally trusting and believing in each other's abilities. It was a credit to Iain's psychological skill and leadership.

I'd probably be the only one in that 11-man team who would be content in a Laser or a Finn. For me, solo sailing is the ultimate. I'm finicky about boat preparation, and having everything working perfectly gives me great pleasure and fulfilment. Then there's the thrill of the contest – no one to blame, no one to share the spoils of victory (or the bitter taste of that other thing).

It's not a sport where you can bask in the spectator spotlight. The journalists and camera crews are flat-out covering the football, the cricket, the baseball. The gratification has to come out of doing your own thing, and not needing to share the experience.

Developing an attitude

Setting goals and achieving them is the surest way to build a winning approach to the sport. The more you attain, the more you want to go on attaining, particularly in this one-man craft. Gratification is addictive, so success is self-perpetuating.

It's important to keep the goals realistic. For me, the simple fact of having sailed well is sufficient, regardless of my placing. Self-analysis can be a hard task-master; to improve, you must want to. Examine yourself honestly and size-up your weaknesses. Accept criticism from people who know; it's better to realise you've got a shortfall, and work on it, than to continue on the road to nowhere.

Ego plays a major part, though sportsmen may be reluctant to admit it. After all, who doesn't fantasise about standing on the podium, revelling in the limelight? Many a highly-motivated person has a healthy ego that needs regular feeding through achievement at sport or business.

Plenty of people delight in bragging about themselves and telling others how things should be done. The mark of a true champion, however, is someone who can keep his ego in check and maintain modesty and graciousness. Ego needn't be a repulsive, all-encompassing monster: in big-fleet Laser racing there is really no place for the gung-ho egomaniac who takes big risks. More often than not it will lead to his demise.

To succeed, you need the statistical adroitness of a mathematician, the analytical dexterity of a scientist, the clinical mentality of a hitman, and perhaps most importantly the conservatism of an accountant. My approach is based on a simple numbers game; there's seven races, nine legs per race, a certain number of boats to defeat. During a race I always try to chip away at the boats in front; making small gains, then getting back to the fleet.

There are gamblers in most fleets, whose hallmark is to take a punt and hit a layline. When it comes off they are temporary heroes, but the odds are generally against them. If you have a hunch that a swing is on its way, go 80 per cent of the way towards benefiting from it to take a handful of boats, rather than 100 per cent in the hope of taking the whole fleet: you may blow it completely.

Obviously, there's a time and a place for taking educated gambles. Being a one-design class, most Lasers

◀ In the Laser class it's just you and the boat, with no-one else to blame . . .

● You need to learn how to sail the boat by instinct and feel, so you can concentrate on what the other boats in the fleet are doing.

are relatively similar in speed, which makes the start and first leg of ultimate importance. Plan your strategy accordingly. If you hold back at the start and get gassed you'll finish 150th. Even a position in the 30s will be virtually impossible to claw back from, so that is the time to take risks.

Strive for an even start, slightly better if you can, and work like crazy for the first quarter of the beat. Get out and get clear. If you do get buried then go for it. You have nothing to lose if you're starting at a poor placing. But you stand a 50:50 chance of achieving a reasonable place by snagging a windshift, hitting a layline or whatever. A 60th is as bad as 160th in the overall scheme, but 20th is a lot better than 60th.

Concentration

At the beginning of the season I have to work hard on my concentration. Specifically, I get involved with things inside the boat when I should be thinking about external matters.

The way to develop concentration is to get the mechanics of the boat down pat. Don't even look at the rig; if the hull feels starved for pressure then second nature should automatically make you ease the cunningham and vang, and maybe slacken the outhaul and sheet.

Of course, this instinct only develops after spending countless training hours in the boat, working at keeping your head out of the boat for longer periods. Ultimately you must be able to make trim adjustments automatically during a race.

There are various things to focus on during a race, according to priorities. Just after the start you obviously want to think about the boats in the vicinity, but the waves could be more important. Cop a bad one at this stage and you're as good as buried, so most of your attention must go to maintaining a smooth passage through the sea.

Once clear, your priority is boatspeed. Concentrate on which of the closest boats warrant attack. As the first beat develops, tactics come more into play. Where are your main opponents? How is the fleet situated? What's the breeze doing?

Race day preparation

I have a structured approach, refined over many years of competition. I like to have my gear sorted out well in advance, leaving my mind free for the racing problems of the day.

Before packing it in the car, I double check everything – clothing, ropes, sail, spars, foils – just to make sure nothing is likely to break.

I tend to get edgy during the morning because of the stress, but since I've done it a huge number of times it's not something that overly concerns me. I know the butterflies will disappear the moment I hit the water.

I don't like to feel rushed, so I get to the regatta site in good time. As I begin the various preparation tasks, maybe extending to polishing the hull, I become quiet, calm and contemplative, a feeling that I try to take into the race.

I rig before most others and get onto the water early to get familiar with the conditions. The only thing on my mind at this stage is the race.

This approach doesn't necessarily work for everyone. I know people who are forever late, who rush around like blue-arsed flies to beg and borrow forgotten items, and can't get motivated unless they're behind the eight ball just to make the start. I can't operate that way, and I'm not convinced it works for too many people.

At foreign regattas, particulary in non-English speaking countries, I examine the sailing instructions thoroughly beforehand then talk them through with another competitor, asking each other pertinent questions.

Basic matters such as boat maintenance and personal well-being must be addressed early to prevent them escalating into major hurdles. At home it's easy; the electric drill fits the socket, the food is familiar. Elsewhere these things take more time to get done.

On the course, people who don't speak the language – or pretend they don't – will use that as a ploy to get away with a port/starboard incident or buoy-room. Always assume they know exactly what's going on and that they're trying a con.

☛ Try to get prepared for the race well in advance so you are calm and in control when the action starts.

Debriefing

While evaluating the race afterwards won't change the outcome, it is invaluable for helping you to improve for the next one. Problems arise in all races, be they tactical or boatspeed oriented, and mistakes are inevitable. Learn from them, and you'll be much the better for it.

At race end I like to distance myself from others around me. It's difficult to talk to me since the events of the day are clocking through my jaded brain. I guess I'm my own worst critic, so if I make an error, particularly one I've made before, it is committed to memory.

By the same token you have to be level-headed about your performance. Some days the breaks don't come your way.

Rectifying mistakes

First you have to recognise what the weaknesses are – usually they occur in patterns – then work them out of your system by training.

Tactical shortfalls are not so easy to amend, since the nous to make instantaneous decisions develops only through race experience. Old campaigners have seen it all and know how to respond instinctively. What a shame you can't put their wisdom into a youthful body.

To cope with setbacks during a race, rationalise them. If they're major then do something about them immediately. Often they can be a source of great inspiration.

When I was 17 I sailed a Youth World Championship in the Moth class. Among the competitors was my best mate, who I'd sat next to at school (we didn't do any work, just doodled boats and their gadgetry endlessly). Going into the final heat of the Worlds only he or I could win. He beat me in the race, and thus took the starry title of Youth Champion.

I remember being shattered for quite some time afterwards. I'd gone into the series confident of winning and becoming this great champion, but all of a sudden he'd stolen the title from underneath me.

Though distressed, I went home and mulled over the events, and finally figured out where my weakness lay. My determination increased two-fold, and happily my mate never beat me again. And I'm pleased to say he's still a mate.

Mental fatigue

The high-pressure environment of championship sailing has cooked the goose of many a sailor. It is quite common for people who've sailed well in the early stages of a regatta to falter through nerves and suffer a catastrophic conclusion, surely the cruellest of blows.

It happened during the first Laser World Championship I won. Come the morning of the crucial seventh heat, it was blowing 30 knots and it seemed likely that the race would be abandoned. I held a narrow points lead at the end of Heat 6 and if the committee decided to scrub the last heat obviously I would've been declared winner.

The natural impulse in this situation is to 'will' an abandonment, but the matter is not in your hands. If you allow yourself to think that way then you'll be at a huge mental disadvantage should the race be declared on.

I worked hard on mental attitude that morning at Falmouth. With the wind screaming across the beach, the mad flapping sound of sailcloth, multiplied more than a 100 times, was almost deafening. Nerves attacked me alright; I'm sure they attacked every competitor, especially the crucial eight who could still take home the title.

I made sure my build-up was as per usual – same rigging ritual, same habits, same positive attitude. I convinced myself that I really wanted to sail the last heat, and when the committee announced "It's on", I had the feeling "Let's do it!"

They say every dog has his day, and this is particularly evident in the fickle sport of Laser racing where things are tight and luck can play a huge part. I know they also say good players make their own luck, but even the best skipper can get hammered without it!

I've found the best way to cope is to keep things in perspective. Think of it as just another boat race; next month or next year there'll be another regatta of the same class. Don't get wound up by it, because that puts undue pressure on your shoulders. My favourite cliché? "It's not life or death."

Superstitions

I once had a cashmere jumper that was exceptionally comfortable and, I was convinced, extremely lucky. I wore it throughout my formative years of sailing, whatever the weather.

Then my father, who used to be superstitious, told me a story about the time he swam at the 1948 Olympics in London. He wore a one-piece costume, the last man in Olympic competition to do so and a far cry from today's swimmers who don lycra and shave their bodies to become more hydrodynamic.

His reasoning was that he'd won the Australian title in the costume, becoming the first Australian to break the one-minute barrier for the 100-metre freestyle in the process. Listening to this as a member of the modern generation, I thought it was absurd that my own Dad would wear a so-called lucky costume! And by the time he'd finished telling me about it he was embarrassed by his own youthful failings.

I immediately committed the cashmere sweater to a life of retirement, and swore never to be superstitious again.

The belief flows into all aspects of sailing. Iain Murray, for example, wouldn't permit even a drop of green paint to be spilled on his 18-foot Skiffs. The best ropes of that era had a green fleck, but he chose another product. Such superstitions go against the grain of getting the most out of yourself and the boat (however, I admit that his ill-fated America's Cupper *Spirit of Australia* had more than just a hint of green on it).

If it's as simple as a favourite cap, then I suppose there can be no harm in it. But tie a piece of string to it so you don't lose the bloody thing!

Psychological warfare

I've never been into playing mind games myself, because I'm not dead sure how to do it. Usually it has the opposite effect to that desired, firing the subject up rather than creating doubt.

There have been only two sailors on the international Laser scene who have tried to erode my confidence with mental ploys, an American and the aforementioned Dutchman. Most of the Yanks are marvellous forthright competitors, a pleasure to be with on and off the water, but there's one who likes to do the termite act. He gets into a situation where you accept him as a training companion, then he uses this proximity to gnaw away at the cerebral framework.

It's easy to fix – just tell these guys you don't enjoy life as much when they're around! The price these people pay is that eventually there are many sailors in a fleet who just don't like them, and who delight in extracting revenge. In short, the psychologies best indulged in are those which you keep as motivational drives inside your own head.

Relationships

The campaign trail can be a bumpy ride for relationships. Emotions run high, and your partner/spouse is often on the receiving end of the associated mood swings.

You may feel on finishing 152nd that you are the same person as the day before, but human nature would suggest differently. If the person understands that and is prepared to be a sounding board then terrific. If not, it's better that they're not around.

The understanding I have with my partner Megan, virtually from the beginning, is that she doesn't come out to watch me on the course.

It dates back to one of my earliest races on Sydney Harbour, where there were several buoys laid for the various classes competing that day. I was leading and nearing the mark when I noticed Megsy waving frantically to me. She was merely saying hello but I thought I'd gone around the wong mark. I waited for other boats to round the mark as confirmation, and almost lost the race.

Back at the beach I threw a bit of a tantrum. She felt I was being vindictive and unfair, so eventually we made a pact that if I was out there to race I didn't want external distractions.

This changed during my third World Championship bid, which I was fortunate enough to wrap up in six heats. On the eve of the seventh heat, possibly my last in serious Laser competition, we decided that Megan could come out. Simultaneously, I made up my mind to take a more cavalier approach to the race: I told her, "I'll either win, or do really badly".

The next day, racing without pressure, the plan came together and I led to the first mark. I could see the spectator craft that Megan was on, and she was hiding behind a canopy with just the lens of her camera poking through. I started to wave and blow kisses at her, and eventually she got the message that everying was OK, and she timidly extracted herself from her hiding place.

This went on every time I rounded the mark, and it cheered me up no end. As it happened, I sailed my best race ever.

Money

I once heard an experienced Australian yachtsman advise: "If you want to practise for the Sydney-Hobart race, try standing under a cold shower tearing up 50-dollar bills". Fortunately Laser sailing doesn't quite fit this description but if you want to campaign overseas, particularly from the Southern Hemisphere, you're going to need some brass.

Budget planning begins before you leave, and make absolutely sure that there's sufficient left at the end to cover any unforeseen problem. If you're doing it on a shoestring budget, then be prepared to enjoy the camaraderie and excitement but don't be disappointed with mediocrity. Character-building as it may be, it only takes a ripped sail or a broken mast to cripple you.

I've known hundreds of would-be champions who start a campaign in fine fettle but, as their financial resources begin to dry up, they skimp on factors that directly effect their well-being. "I won't buy steak tonight, I'll get a pizza instead," they say, so their diets suffer. "I can save 50 bucks by camping in the car tonight" . . . and they suffer sleep deprivation, and can't race properly next day.

Admittedly it can be difficult to obtain an adequate budget; not everyone has wealthy parents! Barring that, private sponsors are tremendous if you're fortunate enough to secure one. Also, fund-raising dinners, club raffles, Government grants, etc. But to get these you really need a track record, so there's a Catch-22 for anyone starting out.

Basically there are no guarantees, other than that you're sure to have a great time.

THE LAST WORD

Reading back over the preceding pages it occurred to me how terribly exacting and demanding it all sounds. It would be remiss of me not to say how much fun it has been.

My first Laser was a 'one-owner, as new' special and it opened the gates to a thousand friendships. Later, when I went to Europe for the first time, I drove around in an absolute bomb of a motor car that dropped a pile of rust with every bump in the road, but it was a great experience.

Racing a tightly-administered one-design class has a certain gladiatorial purity to it – a man-on-man competition with the equipment as identical as it can be. The boat itself is a credit to its designer, having survived a quarter of a century without requiring major changes to embrace contemporary technology.

The exact opposite applies in developmental areas of yachting such as the America's Cup, where technology tips the scales and demands millions be spent. Crew work and sail handling can all be irrelevant if one design computer spits out a better formula than another. There's a contradiction lingering in my mind because, while I enjoyed my time in the America's Cup, I could never accept the concept of different designs providing the ultimate challenge. I guess it's that very notion which determines whether you're cut out for one-design sailing or not.

Looking through the record books, the Laser class has given the world a succession of truly great helmsmen: John Bertrand, Lasse Hjortnaes and Ed Baird to name a few. No doubt the standard will increase as future Laser sailors strive for excellence.

There's a long, long list of great competitors and companions whom I'd like to honour here for the battles fought on the water and for the mutual respect that flowed freely. But as I started to write them down, I realised that there were too many to mention, and that any omission could cause embarrassment.

So to all I just say thanks for the wonderful years.

For a free full-colour brochure write, phone or fax us at:
Fernhurst Books, Duke's Path, High Street, Arundel
West Sussex, BN18 9AJ, UK.
Tel: 01903 882277 Fax: 01903 882715
Email: sales@fernhurstbooks.co.uk
or browse our website:
www.fernhurstbooks.co.uk